STUDIES IN ECONOMIC AND SOCIAL HISTORY

This series, specially commissioned by the Economic History Society, provides a guide to the current interpretations of the key themes of economic and social history in which advances have recently been made or in which there has been significant debate.

Originally entitled 'Studies in Economic History', in 1974 the series had its scope extended to include topics in social history, and the new series title, 'Studies in Economic and Social History', signalises this development.

The series gives readers access to the best work done, helps them to draw their own conclusions in major fields of study, and by means of the critical bibliography in each book guides them in the selection of further reading. The aim is to provide a springboard to further work rather than a set of pre-packaged conclusions or short-cuts.

ECONOMIC HISTORY SOCIETY

The Economic History Society, which numbers over 3000 members, publishes the *Economic History Review* four times a year (free to members) and holds an annual conference. Enquiries about membership should be addressed to the Assistant Secretary, Economic History Society, Peterhouse, Cambridge. Full-time students may join at special rates.

STUDIES IN ECONOMIC AND SOCIAL HISTORY

Edited for the Economic History Society by T. C. Smout

PUBLISHED

OTHER TITLES ARE IN PREPARATION

SOUTH AMERICA
AND THE WORLD ECONOMY
FROM INDEPENDENCE TO
1930

Prepared for
The Economic History Society by

BILL ALBERT
Lecturer in Economic and Social History
University of East Anglia

M

First published 1983 by
THE MACMILLAN PRESS LTD
London and Basingstoke

Companies and representatives
throughout the world

ISBN O 333 34223 2

Printed in Hong Kong

Contents

List of Tables and Maps

Acknowledgements

I would like to thank Bill Mathew for struggling through two drafts of this pamphlet and giving me constant encouragement as well as the benefit of his considerable historical sense and insight. I also owe debts of gratitude for detailed criticisms to Dr Richard Wilson, Dr Peter Blanchard, Dr Colin Lewis, Dr Rory Miller, Paul Henderson, Professor A. G. Hopkins, Miss Sally Forster, and my students.

Note on References

References in the text within square brackets relate to the items in the Bibliography, followed, where necessary, by the page numbers in italics, for example [Platt, 1980, *127*]. Other references in the text, numbered consecutively throughout the book, relate to annotations of the text or to sources not given in the Bibliography, and are itemised in the Notes and References section.

Editor's Preface

SINCE 1968, when the Economic History Society and Macmillan published the first of the 'Studies in Economic and Social History', the series has established itself as a major teaching tool in universities, colleges and schools, and as a familiar landmark in serious bookshops throughout the country. A great deal of the credit for this must go to the wise leadership of its first editor, Professor M. W. Flinn, who retired at the end of 1977. The books tend to be bigger now than they were originally, and inevitably more expensive; but they have continued to provide information in modest compass at a reasonable price by the standards of modern academic publications.

There is no intention of departing from the principles of the first decade. Each book aims to survey findings and discussion in an important field of economic or social history that has been the subject of recent lively debate. It is meant as an introduction for readers who are not themselves professional researchers but who want to know what the discussion is all about — students, teachers and others generally interested in the subject. The authors, rather than either taking a strongly partisan line or suppressing their own critical faculties, set out the arguments and the problems as fairly as they can, and attempt a critical summary and explanation of them from their own judgement. The discipline now embraces so wide a field in the study of the human past that it would be inappropriate for each book to follow an identical plan, but all volumes will normally contain an extensive descriptive bibliography.

The series is not meant to provide all the answers but to help readers to see the problems clearly enough to form their own conclusions. We shall never agree in history, but the discipline will be well served if we know what we are disagreeing about, and why.

T. C. SMOUT

University of St Andrews   *Editor*

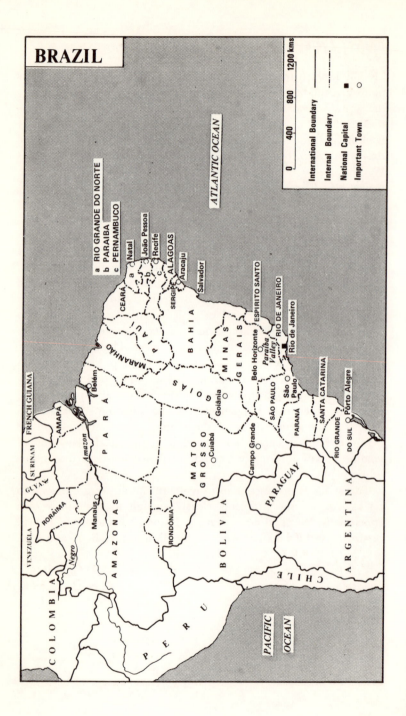

ARGENTINA

PARAGUAY

JUJUY

Salta

S A L T A

FORMOSA

CHACO

MISIONES

San Miguel de Tucumán

CATAMARCA

SANTIAGO

Santiago
del Estero

Resistencia

Corrientes

BRAZIL

Catamarca

DEL ESTERO

CORRIENTES

L A
RIOJA

SANTA
FÉ

C H I L E

SAN
JUAN

Córdoba

Santa Fé

Paraná

CÓRDOBA

Mendoza

SAN

Río Cuarto

Rosario

ENTRE
RÍOS

URUGUAY

MENDOZA

LUIS

Pergamino

San Rafael

Buenos Aires

Montevideo

B U E N O S
A I R E S

L A
PAMPA

Bahía Blanca

Mar del
Plata

NEUQUEN

R Í O
N E G R O

ATLANTIC OCEAN

C H U B U T

Comodoro Rivadavia

S A N T A
C R U Z

| 0 | 160 | 320 | 480 kms. |

International Boundary

Internal Boundary

National Capital ■

Important Town ○

Río Gallegos

TIERRA
DEL
FUEGO

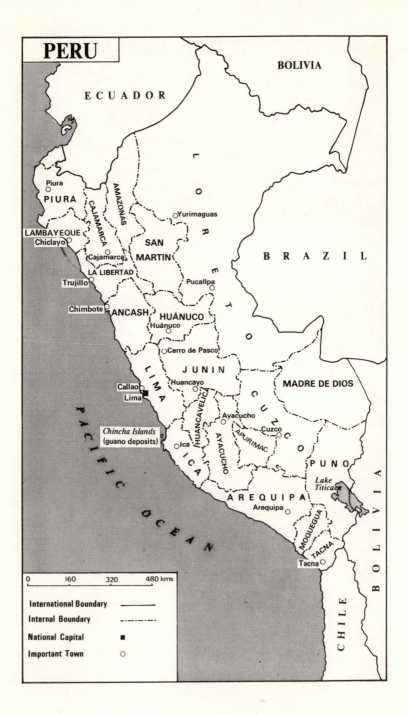

PERU

BOLIVIA

ECUADOR

L
O
R
E
T
O

BRAZIL

Piura
PIURA

AMAZONAS

CAJAMARCA

Yurimaguas

LAMBAYEQUE
Chiclayo

Cajamarca

SAN
MARTIN

LA LIBERTAD

Trujillo

Pucallpa

Chimbote   ANCASH   HUÁNUCO
Huánuco

Cerro de Pasco

L
I
M
A

JUNIN

MADRE DE DIOS

Callao
Lima

Huancayo

C
U
Z
C
O

HUANCAVELICA

Ayacucho

Cuzco

Chincha Islands
(guano deposits)

Ica

AYACUCHO

APURIMAC

PUNO

I
C
A

Lake
Titicaca

AREQUIPA

B
O
L
I
V
I
A

Arequipa

P
A
C
I
F
I
C

O
C
E
A
N

MOQUEGUA

TACNA

Tacna

0   160   320   480 kms

International Boundary ⎯⎯⎯

Internal Boundary ⎯·⎯·⎯

National Capital   ■

Important Town   ○

C
H
I
L
E

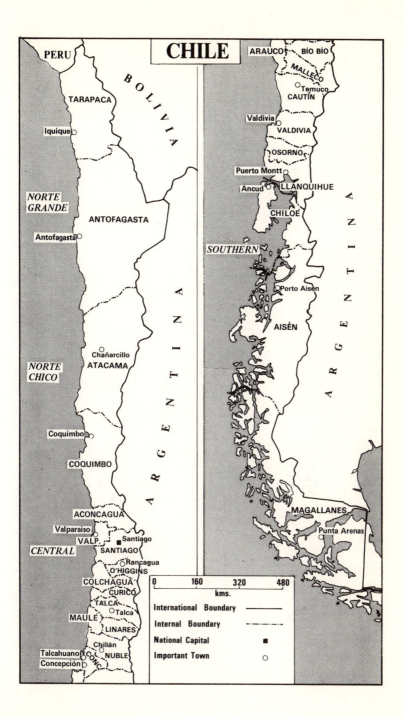

CHILE

PERU

BOLIVIA

ARGENTINA

TARAPACA

Iquique○

NORTE GRANDE

ANTOFAGASTA

Antofagasta○

NORTE CHICO

Chañarcillo○
ATACAMA

Coquimbo○

COQUIMBO

ACONCAGUA

Valparaiso○

VALP. ■ Santiago

CENTRAL **SANTIAGO**

○Rancagua
O'HIGGINS

COLCHAGUA

CURICÓ

TALCA ○Talca

MAULE

LINARES

○Chillán
Talcahuano○ **ÑUBLE**
Concepción○ CONC.

ARAUCO **BÍO BÍO**

MALLECO

○Temuco
CAUTÍN

Valdivia○

VALDIVIA

OSORNO

Puerto Montt○

Ancud○ **LLANQUIHUE**

CHILOÉ

SOUTHERN

○Porto Aisén

AISÉN

MAGALLANES

Punta Arenas○

0	160	320	480

kms.

International Boundary ——————

Internal Boundary - - - - - - -

National Capital ■

Important Town ○

Introduction

IN this book an outline is presented of some of the main debates concerning how economic development in South America was influenced by the area's links with the world economy from the early decades of the nineteenth century to the onset of the Great Depression. Mexico, Central America and the Caribbean are largely excluded from the analysis because limitation of space make adequate coverage impossible. The economic history of South America is approached from the standpoint of the area's connections with the international economy because export growth, foreign investment, immigration and the transfer of technology were such dominating features of the period for most countries. Not surprisingly many of the most critical historical debates revolve around the question of the impact of these external forces on the national economies. However, it must not be imagined that by concentrating on exogenous factors the economic history of this vast and complex continent will be fully revealed. Despite strong elements of a common colonial heritage, each country experienced a quite distinctive historical evolution. An appreciation of this distinctiveness is of overriding importance in understanding the course of economic and social change in the different countries. In short, what follows is not a survey of the economic history of South America but only an introduction to one of the key aspects of that varied history.

The book consists of three main parts. In the first the differing theoretical approaches to the study of Latin American economic development are considered. This is followed by an account of the principal changes in the area's external economic relations over the period. The final section is made up of four case studies in which some of the general questions raised in the previous sections are examined more closely. Brazil, Argentina, Peru and Chile have been selected because of the instructive contrasts provided by the distinctive patterns of their export-led growth. It should be noted that because this work is written essentially for the non-specialist, references to works in Spanish and Portuguese have been kept to an absolute minimum, although guidance to such sources is provided in the Bibliography.

15

1 Approaches to the Study of Latin American Economic History in the Post-Colonial Period

THE economic history of colonial Latin America has received considerable scholarly attention, but the nineteenth and twentieth centuries have not been as well served until quite recently. One reason for this is that the running of the highly centralised, bureaucratic Spanish and Portuguese empires generated a much greater quantity of documentation than the briefer and more chaotic national period. It has also been suggested by Stein [Cortés Conde and Stein, 1977] that until the Great Depression there was relatively little modern economic history written because what had sparked off such research in the more advanced countries – the far-reaching changes associated with the industrial revolution – had not occurred here. Furthermore, before 1929 substantive critical analysis was limited because it was widely believed by most observers that Latin America would follow the path of development mapped out by the industrialised countries, or at least develop by exploiting its supposed comparative advantage in the production of primary commodities within the world economy. All this changed with the collapse of that economy in the 1930s, a collapse which had a profound impact on Latin America and indicated not only that export dependency was risky but also that there was no common or well-charted path to development. From this period a growing concern with the many obstacles to development has fostered a greater interest in the area's economic history. The approaches to this history have been strongly influenced in turn by changing and conflicting conceptions of the development process.

The writing of all history is based on certain assumptions about the laws of economic and social change, assumptions which are derived implicitly or explicitly from various theoretical formulations of the dynamics of such change. It is therefore necessary to begin by outlining some major categories of development theory which have influenced and informed the study of Latin America's modern economic history. These theories, formulated by economists, sociologists and political scientists to explain the phenomenon of underdevelopment are not only varied and numerous, but also concern themselves with an immensely wide range of issues. What follows concentrates on only one, albeit possibly the most important,

17

of these – the relationship between advanced and backward economies.

The general conception of economic development which until quite recently has exercised the greatest influence on historians is that often labelled as 'diffusionist'. This category embraces models of development which differ in many fundamental respects but generally share the basic assumption that all areas of the world were at one time underdeveloped and that this condition can be altered by breaking down those traditional economic, social and political structures which stand in the way of progress. To do this the growth of exports, the development of transport systems, and such factors as imports of foreign capital, expertise, technology, labour, and so on, are seen as having a vital catalytic role. While many writers are critical of certain aspects of foreign involvement, it is argued that such involvement has been broadly beneficial and helpful to the modernisation of the third world [Chilcote and Edelstein, 1974].

The variation of approach and emphasis within the broad diffusionist framework is so extreme, ranging from Karl Marx to W. W. Rostow (author of *The Stages of Economic Growth: A Non-Communist Manifesto*), that it is impossible to pick a single author as representative. None the less, among liberal economic historians Rostow's ideas, particularly his general conception of economic change, have had a pervasive and lasting impact and should therefore be noted. He maintains that economic development proceeds by a series of stages from traditional society through a period of establishing preconditions for growth to the watershed of 'take-off' and beyond to maturity and high mass consumption. In this process the relationship between the developed and underdeveloped world is one in which the latter benefits from the example and the assistance of the former. Although very influential, his work has been comprehensively criticised by fellow liberal economists, and this, plus the fact that there are many other diffusionist models of development, suggests that care must be taken by critics who choose Rostow as epitomising the diffusionist perspective. This can, and often does, lead to the setting up of an easily destroyed straw man.

The provenance of the current radical critique of development theory is not to be found specifically in a dissatisfaction with the liberal bias of that theory, although it strongly rejects this, but rather in the perceived failure of earlier attempts to provide an

18

alternative to the neo-classical model of development. A central tenet of this model is that countries will progress through exploiting their comparative advantage in the world market, for example the developed countries providing industrial goods in exchange for the primary products of the rest of the world. A refutation of this theory was formulated in the late 1940s by economists at the Economic Commission for Latin America (ECLA) led by Raul Prebisch, their work drawing on Latin America's long-standing nationalist, anti-imperialist, though non-Marxist, traditions. They claimed that underdevelopment was the result of Latin America's inferior position within the international economy. The terms of trade (the ratio of export to import prices) had for decades moved against the primary producers and the region faced a long-term structural crisis in its balance of payments. For this and other reasons they argued for import-substitution industrialisation behind tariff barriers. Externally orientated, export-dependent efforts were to give way to more internally directed national policies [O'Brien, 1975; Chilcote and Edelstein, 1974].

The apparent failure of the ECLA prescription to cure Latin America's economic ills provoked the more radical dependency approach, of which a number of distinct and often conflicting variants have been put forward. It is impossible here to do justice to the voluminous and acrimonious debate over the issue of dependency, and what follows is selective, concentrating on those points which relate directly to the problem of South America's external links.

One of the most significant breaks made by the *dependentistas* (foreshadowed in the ECLA analysis) with liberal development theory is the denial that underdevelopment is a traditional state. Instead it is argued that development in the metropolitan countries and underdevelopment in the third world are intimately related aspects of the same historical process – the growth and expansion of the world capitalist system. The structures which obstruct progressive change are not, therefore, traditional but ones created during and since the colonial era to facilitate Latin America's integration and subordination within the international economy. Development is stifled as these structures are used by the metropolis to expropriate the surplus generated in the peripheral economies. As André Gunder Frank, perhaps the best-known proponent of this thesis, writes, 'it is capitalism, both world and national, which

19

produced underdevelopment in the past and which still generates underdevelopment in the present' [Frank, 1969]. Very few within the dependency school would now agree with Frank's stagnationist argument, and indeed virtually every aspect of his work has been challenged. There would, however, probably be broad agreement with O'Brien's comment that 'theories of dependency are trying to show that the internal dynamics of Latin American society and its underdevelopment was and is primarily conditioned by Latin America's position within the international economy, and the resultant ties between internal and external structures' [13].

To sum up the argument so far, of all the many differences between the diffusionist and dependency approaches perhaps the most fundamental, particularly in terms of this essay, is over the nature of the relationship between the industrialised countries and the third world. In broad terms exponents of the dependency thesis see this relationship as one of domination and exploitation and argue that through the colonial and national periods it has been responsible for creating structural underdevelopment. On the other hand, the diffusionists contend that underdevelopment is essentially an endogenous problem and that progressive transformation has been and will be stimulated by the multiplicity of contacts with the international economy. These opposing views are derived from fairly irreconcilable ideological positions. Whereas the diffusionist argument seems to proceed from the premise that the extension of capitalism is needed for development, most *dependentistas* advocate a socialist alternative as the only hope for progressive change in Latin America.

For the writing of Latin American economic history the debates over theories of development have yielded useful new insights as well as much confusion and useless polemic. In offering a radical alternative to liberal development theory the notion of dependency has at least forced historians to examine their assumptions about the process of economic and social change. Furthermore, the provocative questions raised by the new approach, for example about the existence of traditional economic structures or the role of foreign trade and investment, have served to stimulate and generally inform much valuable historical research. At the same time uncertainty over definitions and historical methods have resulted in many confused, muddled and consequently rather sterile debates. One reason for this is that most dependency theorists employ dubious historical methodology, consisting of an uncritical reliance on selected secondary sources and a tendency to use 'historical facts' to fill in a rigidly predetermined framework. There is often no dialectical relationship set up between evidence and theory, and so as historical work *per se* much dependency analysis is of questionable value. However, *dependentistas* defend themselves, somewhat disingenuously, by claiming that they are not trying to write history. For example, O'Brien comments that 'the theory of dependency is not meant to offer an economic history of Latin America, but rather a perspective within which to analyse that history' [*19*]. Not surprisingly, many historians, already predisposed to be suspicious of theory and of social science, have found this a less than satisfactory defence for the use of what they see as slipshod methods [Platt, 1980].

Criticisms of method may be justifiable in terms of the empirical traditions within which most historical studies are conceived, but such criticisms may also be misplaced because some dependency theorists are working within an entirely different tradition. For example, Cardoso argues that it is wrong to freeze dependency analysis, as some writers have done, into a formal theory with distinct, testable propositions simply to meet either Marxist or empiricist objections. He writes,[1]

> this kind of definition of the notion of dependency also modifies the theoretical field of its study; instead of making dialectical analysis of historical processes, conceiving of them as the result of struggles of classes and groups that define their interests and values in the process of the expansion of a mode of production, history is formalized; the specific contributions that these analyses of dependency might make from a methodological point of view (that is the idea of contradiction) is withdrawn.

There is, in short, an almost unbridgeable epistemological divide not only between the diffusionist and dependency camps but also among dependency theorists themselves. While they may discuss the same general issues, in this instance the historical dimensions of development/underdevelopment, this does not mean there is always sufficient agreement about what these issues are for there to be grounds for genuine debate.

To what extent Latin America's economic development was conditioned or determined by outside pressures perforce raises the question of how these pressures were brought into play. It has long been accepted by many Latin American writers, as well as radical foreign critics that the new states were the victims of an aggressive imperialist onslaught, led first by Britain and then by the United States. Leaving aside these countries' extensive economic interests in the area, the claim of imperialist coercion, in the sense of the use of force, seems amply supported by the United States' long record of armed and diplomatic intervention, particularly in Mexico, Central America and the Caribbean, and Britain's more than forty military adventures in Latin America between 1880 and 1914. In the case of Britain (for the purposes of this study the more important of the two) it has been argued that armed incursions were extremely transitory affairs and that the claims of 'informal' imperialist domination have been overstated, with regard to both official government policy and economic control. With reference to the former Platt observes,[2]

> official demands on behalf of British interests overseas never went beyond equal favour and open competition: non-intervention in the internal affairs of foreign states was one of the most respected principles of British diplomacy .... [The government was always reluctant] to extend its responsibilities beyond the minimum required to guarantee the free play of the market, the normal interaction of supply and demand.

While it is important to examine with care the role of foreign government or business in Latin America, if it is found that undue pressure or unfair practices were not employed in any particular case, as for example Mathew concludes in his study of Peru during the Guano Age (see below, pp. 71–2), this in itself does not mean that the economies of these countries were not shaped, dominated or exploited by foreign interests. To assume that it does is to accept the idea that there was something neutral or natural about the functioning of the international economy. It is precisely this point which the dependency thesis attacks, arguing that it was essentially through the normal working of a world economy dominated by the industrial powers that Latin America's economies were subordinated to the former's interests and their progressive development thwarted.

There is no simple way to cut through the analytical tangle outlined above and provide a simple, clear standard for assessing the many debates over Latin American development in these years. One important reason for this is that there is little agreement over exactly what constitutes development. Diffusionists tend to measure this in terms of increasing per-capita Gross National Product (GNP) and evidence of social and political 'modernisation'. On the other hand, the dependency school argues that most underdeveloped countries have experienced economic growth but not development. In defining the latter they stress, among other things, the need for structural changes leading to national economic sovereignty and a degree of economic and political equality [Chilcote and Edelstein, 1974, *4, 28*]. Therefore the construction of railways, which one writer will argue was a positive change because it contributed towards increasing productive capacity, will be seen by another as primarily a means by which a country's export-dependence was strengthened and its structural underdevelopment thereby enhanced. This weighing up of the costs and benefits of economic transformation demands judgement for which no blueprint can be offered. This is not, however, to suggest that all historical interpretations are equally valid. Some, for example, are logically inconsistent and/or based on inadequate empirical research. Also, the choice of certain issues as historically significant in explaining an historical problem is always open to criticism. This is especially true when the problem is as complex and contentious as the relationship between Latin America and the world economy in a period of more than one hundred years. Some of the principal components of that relationship, that is trade, investment, export sectors, foreign control and immigration, are outlined below. But, important as they are, it must be stressed that they represent only pieces of the very much more elaborate puzzle of economic, social, political and cultural change experienced by an extremely diverse group of countries.

2 Latin America and the World Economy from Independence to 1930: An Overview

IT is impossible here to give the reader even a feeling for the extent and complexity of Latin America's links with the international economy and the effects these had on development in the period under review. What follows is a very brief account of those points of external contact through which the most profound influence on economic change in the republics was exercised. This survey will provide general background for the more detailed consideration of these issues in the four case studies. For ease of exposition, a rough periodisation has been adopted. The years to 1880, of nation-building and generally slow export growth, will be considered separately from the subsequent period of more dramatic export expansion. Exports have been identified as the pivotal variable, it being broadly agreed that the period 1880–1930 was a time when most countries experienced a greater or lesser degree of export-led growth. The main point in dispute is whether or not this growth of exports led to wider progressive change in Latin America.

INDEPENDENCE TO 1880

Napoleon's conquests in the Iberian Peninsula (1807–8) set in motion a chain of events which were to lead to independence for most of Latin America. In November 1807, the Portuguese royal family fled from the French invaders to Brazil aboard a British warship. When in 1821 King Dom Joao returned with his court to Lisbon, his son Dom Pedro remained to become, a year later, the first emperor of an independent Brazil. By forcing the abdication of the Spanish Bourbons in 1808, Napoleon's armies also shattered central authority in Spain. This in turn was to spark off a series of rebellions in Spanish America, led by the American-born (creole) elite and lasting from about 1810 to 1824. Creole discontent with Spanish domination was long-standing. It had been increasing from the latter decades of the eighteenth century as Spain attempted to counter the growing commercial and military threat posed by other European powers, particularly Britain, by instituting a series of major reforms intended both to revitalise the colonial economies and to place them more firmly under her control. The result was that the creoles gained in economic strength but did not have the political power to develop that strength as they saw fit. None the less, until the war-induced crisis forced their hand, their desire for independence had been outweighed by their fear of unleashing popular unrest and endangering the hierarchical social order upon which their economic position depended.

The break with Spain and Portugal did not, however, bring with it any immediate changes in existing social and economic structures, Latin America's 'colonial heritage'. For the great mass of the people, the Indians, *mestizos* and black slaves, independence meant very little as they continued, in most cases, to be ruled by a small white elite. At the same time, it is widely argued that formal colonialism was replaced by informal British control, the consequence of Latin America being drawn more firmly into the international economy which Britain dominated. The Steins present a fairly representative view when they write, 'The English had been the major factor in the destruction of Iberian imperialism; on its ruins they erected the informal imperialism of free trade and investment' [Stein and Stein, 1970, *155*]. Platt has strongly objected to this: 'the break with Spain,' he maintains, 'far from confirming the integration of Latin America as a dependent partner in the world economy, reintroduced an unwelcome half century of "independence" from foreign trade and investment' [Platt, 1980, *127*). This controversy, rooted in a basic disagreement about the dynamics of the world capitalist system and, more prosaically, about the use of words, also has much to do with questions of dating, emphasis and the continual problem of making generalisations about such a vast and diverse area. None the less, it is possible to deal separately with a number of issues raised by this debate:

1) the impact of European imports on Latin American producers;
2) the possible alternatives to externally oriented development; and
3) the importance of foreign investment and exports for the various economies.

It is clear that during and immediately after the war years, because of the need for diplomatic recognition, loans and trade, Britain exercised substantial economic and political influence in Latin America. This was particularly true in Brazil, where treaties signed before and after independence (1810, 1827) granted preferential tariffs to British goods (see below, pp. 43–4). In the rest of Latin America the opening of the ports led to a flood of imports, merchants believing that a vast market would be found. The myth of an untapped El Dorado also encouraged a short-lived (1822–5) investment mania, during which about £25 to £30 million (nominal capital) was raised, mainly by the British for mining ventures and government loans. Both trade and investment soon came to grief in the chaos of the post-colonial period. Most loans were in default by the mid-1820s and markets were quickly overstocked. This was hardly surprising, for the long years of war had left a legacy of devastation: Spanish capital withdrawn, labour systems and trade routes disrupted, mines flooded and agricultural land abandoned. Recovery was made more difficult by the violent political conflicts within and between the new nations which engulfed most of the area for decades after independence. Because of these and other related problems, the claim that local handicraft production was undermined by cheap foreign imports and that export dependence was thereby encouraged has probably been exaggerated. On this point Halperín writes,

> The inflow of imported low-cost goods was a very heavy blow to certain sectors of local production, particularly agriculture and handicrafts, but its effects were felt more gradually and partially than the apocalyptic versions of today's critics would have us believe. [Halperín, 1973, *51*]

Whether or not artisanal production was disrupted or eliminated by foreign competition, somewhat surprisingly there seems fairly broad agreement that scant basis existed in Latin America for domestically generated economic development. The elements needed for this, such as capital, skilled labour, transport, banking and markets, were either scarce or non-existent. Diffusionists tend to argue, as did Latin American liberals at the time, that these deficiencies could be made good by fuller, freer contact with the international economy. On the other hand, *dependentistas* maintain that it was precisely because of the external economic orientation throughout the colonial period that institutional underdevelopment was a problem. New foreign ties, particularly with Britain, made this problem more intractable, reinforcing the more retrograde features of the area's colonial heritage.

Despite the emphasis placed on the influence of colonial institutions, the impression is given, especially by Frank, that in the post-independence period there were other paths to development in Latin America besides that offered by the world economy. In most countries there were in fact groups who favoured some form of locally based development. In Colombia and Mexico, for example, attempts were made to encourage industry with tariffs and special concessions, while in Chile similar measures were part of a broader policy of state-directed development (see below, pp. 78–9). The most dramatic and oft-cited example of an alternative model of development is that of Paraguay. This landlocked nation was purposely cut off from the international economy by its first ruler, Dr Francia, until his death in 1840, and only cautiously opened up by his successors. Opinion over the significance of the Paraguayan experience could not be more divided. Frank sees the government here as the most 'popular' in Latin America [Frank, 1972, *52–3*]. White concurs with this assessment and observes,[3]

> Unlike its semi-independent, neocolonial sister states, whose dependent economies served to enrich the local elite and the capitalist world metropolises, Paraguay, by establishing an autonomous economic as well as political system, had truly won its full independence.

Lynch disagrees with this, maintaining that under Francia's 'pseudo-populist dictatorship' there was economic stagnation and no social change [Lynch, 1973]. While this question demands far closer analysis, it is important to note that throughout Latin America the groups opposing freer trade were generally those most concerned with preserving the established social and political order. They seem, therefore, a dubious choice for leaders of progressive national development, notwithstanding the possible benefits of their economic policies.

By about mid-century in most countries the 'nationalist' programme had been abandoned in favour of a more open, export-based development formula. Experience varied greatly, but a prime reason underlying this change was the steady growth in the demand for primary commodities caused by the expansion of industrial capitalism in Europe. This in turn stimulated a modest, but significant, degree of export growth as well as a return of foreign capital to Latin America. Venezuela, a country most severely affected by the wars of independence, was one of the first to recover and showed a rapid growth in coffee and cattle exports from the 1830s. Chilean copper and silver production rose steadily until the 1960s, and wheat exports were also buoyant (see below, pp. 76–7). A rapid increase in Colombia's tobacco exports (1850–75) offered, but in the end did not provide, escape from decades of economic stagnation. In the hinterland of Rio de Janeiro the coffee frontier was being extended from the 1820s, and this process spread to São Paulo in the 1860s. Argentina's pastoral exports, especially wool, were making significant advances, and Peru between 1840 and 1880 experienced possibly the most dramatic growth of the period with export booms, first in guano and later in nitrates. The Peruvian case is instructive because a principal reason for the apparently tremendous success of guano as an export was that its extraction was so primitive, by shovels wielded by indentured Chinese coolies. No sophisticated transport or commercial infrastructure was needed as the deposits were located on small off-shore islands (see below, p. 70). Most of Latin America's other exports had to wait for the extension of railway systems, begun in the 1860s and 1870s, before their potential could be fully exploited.

Foreign investors, suspicious of Latin America after the crash of 1826, began to regain a degree of confidence, particularly from the 1850s. Loans from Britain (overwhelmingly the most important source) rose from about £30 million in 1826 to £80.8 million by 1865, £26.5 being new securities and the rest arrears and conversions of previous loans. The period of most rapid increase was 1860–5, when two-thirds of these new loans were raised. Mexico and Brazil were the most important borrowers and government loans accounted for 76 per cent of the total. In the next decade (see Table I) British investment in Latin America more than doubled; Peru, because of the attraction of her guano and nitrate wealth, took the largest single share.

In summary, it cannot be maintained that Latin American independence ushered in fifty years of isolation from the international economy. Besides the many instances of European and US military and diplomatic intervention (particularly in Mexico, Central America, Brazil and Argentina), the peaceful but more pervasive ties of trade and investment were also extended and made

Table I

British Investment (accumulated) in Latin American Governments and Railways 1865 and 1875 (£000)

	1865			1875		
	Govt	*Rails*	*Total*	*Govt*	*Rails*	*Total*
Argentina	2206	512	2718	16,490	5054	21,544
Brazil	13,036	5375	18,411	20,355	6362	26,717
Chile	2253	658	2911	8274	1378	9652
Colombia	7340	–	7340	2094	1170	3264
Mexico	23,541	600	24,141	23,541	3360	26,901
Peru	3698	206	3904	33,535	2540	36,075
Venezuela	6224	–	6224	6809	550	7359
Others	3483	2200	5683	18,262	3671	21,933
Total	61,781	9551	71,332	129,360	24,085	153,445
Other investments			9537			21,166
Total investments			80,869			174,611

Source: Stone, 1968, pp. 323, 325, 329. Much government borrowing was undertaken to finance railway building.

firmer. This in turn strengthened the position of those in Latin America who saw economic progress in terms of freer trade, foreign capital and the growth of exports. This pattern of development, so clearly established in these years, was to be greatly elaborated upon from the 1880s.

1880–1930

The period 1880–1930 can be broadly characterised as one in which the continued expansion of industrial capitalism generated a complex of forces which resulted in the bonds linking Latin America to the world economy being forged with greater strength. Together with population growth, the development of the forces of production in the metropolitan countries gave rise to an increased demand for food and raw materials. This development also involved a series of major, interrelated, technical breakthroughs which made it possible to produce, and more importantly to distribute (steamships, railways, telegraph), a vastly increased volume of primary commodities. Underpinning this process was a massive upsurge in the flow of capital and labour across the Atlantic. In what follows some of the principal aspects of this process are briefly discussed in order to provide the background needed for the more detailed studies of individual countries. Over these years there were significant discontinuities, and it is therefore useful to divide the period into three main sub-periods:

1) 1880–1914 – the 'golden age' of the international economy when export-led growth was most dramatic;
2) the interregnum of the first world war;
3) the 1920s, a time of fundamental transition with the United States replacing Britain as the dominant economic force in Latin America and in the world economy.

Attention will be focused here primarily on the first phase of development, the latter two being considered briefly at the end of the section.

EXPORTS

Stimulated by changes in the international economy, exports from most Latin American countries exhibited vigorous expansion in the decades before the first world war (Table II), these years, together

Table II

Annual Rate of Growth of Exports 1883–1913 (in current US dollars)

Cuba	2.9%	Ecuador	5.1%
Brazil	4.5%	Colombia	4.1%
Venezuela	1.3%	Argentina	7.6%
Peru	3.7%	Chile	2.1%
Mexico	4.3%	Uruguay	3.6%
Central America	3.7%		

Source: W. Arthur Lewis, *Growth and Fluctuations 1870–1913* (London, 1978) pp. 196, 203.

with those to 1930, being labelled as the classic period of *desarrollo hacia afuera* – externally oriented development. The figures in Table II show that the intensity of growth varied, but they do not show the equally important differences in take-off dates and fluctuations in rates of export growth over time. For example, the Colombian coffee boom is generally dated from about 1910, and in Peru the value of exports did not begin to rise until 1896, increasing from then until 1913 by 7.5 per cent. per year. In Chile the two decades from 1890 saw exports rise by 9.3 and 7 per cent respectively, and in Brazil a 4.7 per cent growth rate from the early 1880s to the mid-1890s was halved in the subsequent years up to the first world war. The differences between these figures and those given in Table II are due to the former being measured in depreciating local currency. None the less, they do give a reasonable indication of exporters' increasing earnings.

Despite the substantial growth in export earnings Prebisch has claimed that because of a secular decline in the terms of trade Latin America increasingly had to sell more in order to obtain the same quantity of imports.[4] In this way, it is argued, wealth was siphoned off to the industrialised countries and relative economic disparities reinforced. This view is challenged by Schneider [1981] who maintains that between 1826 and 1856 Latin America's terms of trade with France improved, mainly because of increased industrial productivity. This was also probably true with respect to Britain, although from the 1860s the terms of trade did move in her favour.[5] However, because of problems of measurement it is not clear whether this meant that the terms of trade moved against Latin America. For example, Peláez [1976] has shown that in the period 1857–1906 Brazil's terms of trade improved markedly. Whether this was true for other Latin American countries remains to be established.

It is interesting to note that, with the exception of Cuba and the coffee producers Brazil and Venezuela, most countries experienced a change from the earlier decades of the century in their principal export (Table III). This indicates important changes in the structure of domestic production. There were significant differences in the commodity composition of exports, and in the degree of specialisation: Cuba, Brazil and Chile showing a much narrower export base than either Argentina or Peru. Among other things, this tended to make the latter countries relatively less vulnerable both to specific adverse price movements and to regional economic imbalance, a more diverse export mix generally being associated with a wider geographical spread of production. The type of commodity produced is also important in that the associated technical considerations and form of productive organisation may have had a significant effect on the export's potential for inducing more widespread economic transformation. Plantation production, for example, is generally viewed as not being conducive to progressive social or economic change, given that it is often associated with direct foreign control, extreme income inequality, inefficient use of land, dependence on large numbers of unskilled workers, and isolation from the rest of the economy.[6]

Table III

Commodity Composition of Exports

Argentina	(1910–14)	Wheat 19.4%, Maize 17.9%, Linseed 10.2%, Hides 11%, Wool 12.9%, Frozen Beef 7.9%
Brazil	(1908–12)	Coffee 54.2%, Rubber 27.9%
Chile	(1910–13)	Nitrates and Iodine 86%, Copper 8%
Peru	(1910–13)	Sugar 17.5%, Cotton 13.8%, Copper 20.5%, Petroleum 6.3%, Rubber 12.3%
Mexico	(1910–11)	Gold 18%, Silver 27%, Henequen 8.5%, Copper 9%, Rubber 7%
Colombia	(1910–14)	Coffee 46%, Metals 19%, Bananas 9%, Hides 9%
Cuba	(1914)	Sugar 77%, Tobacco 16%
Venezuela	(1908–12)	Coffee 52%, Cocoa 16.6%

Sources: Albert and Henderson, 1981; F. Norbury, 'Venezuela', in W. A. Lewis (ed.), *Tropical Development, 1880–1913* (London, 1970) p. 129; W. McGreevey, *An Economic History of Colombia, 1845–1930* (Cambridge, 1971) p. 207; *The Mexican Yearbook 1912* (London, 1913) p. 10; *The Cane Sugar Industry*, US Dept of Commerce, Misc. Series no. 53, 1917, p. 357.

In terms of the wider impact of exports, the extent of foreign ownership is a key issue. This is because capital accumulation is the *sine qua non* of capitalist development, and if export sectors are in foreign hands it is more likely that profits will be accumulated abroad. In Latin America the incidence of direct outside control of this kind varied considerably. In Chile, Cuba, Mexico and Peru, for example, there was a significant degree of foreign ownership of nitrate workings, sugar estates, mines, petroleum, and so on, much of this intensifying after 1900. In Colombia, Brazil and Argentina, on the other hand, the productive system remained primarily under national control. A related issue is the type of indirect foreign control exercised in the commercialisation of exports. Here all countries were in a somewhat similar position. The commercial infrastructure needed to operate the export sectors was largely dominated by foreign merchant houses and banks (mainly British). At times this was associated with a marked degree of oligopoly, for example by about 1900 60 per cent of Brazil's coffee was shipped by six or seven firms. The probity of the merchants and the extent of their power and control remain issues of debate [Greenhill, 1977], but there is little doubt that their overall influence was massive as it was they who spun the web by which Latin America was so firmly enmeshed within the international economy.

FOREIGN INVESTMENT

Foreign investment in Latin America began to pick up from the 1860s. There were distinct fluctuations over time, but the increase from the third quarter of the century was spectacular, the amount rising to nearly £2000 million by the first world war (Table IV), about 20 per cent of the world's total. Britain remained the single most important source of capital, although from the turn of the century France, Germany and the United States began to assume more prominent roles. There was also a marked increase in the share of investment going into railways and public utilities. Railway mileage in Latin America rose from 7500 miles in 1880, to 34,480 in 1900 to 63,000 twenty years later. Argentina, Brazil and Mexico

Table IV

Foreign Investment (accumulated) in Latin America 1913 and 1929 (£000) *

	1913					1929	
	UK	US	France	Germany	Total	UK	US
Argentina	492,893	8214	82,135	41,068	624,310	439,446	125,560
Brazil	257,323	10,267	143,737	102,670	513,997	209,265	97,750
Chile	71,458	3080	10,267	–	84,805	80,030	81,260
Peru	37,696	7187	–	20,535	65,418	28,930	30,983
Mexico	115,051	164,271	82,135	–	361,457	212,462	318,295
Colombia	9922	411			(10,333)	7780	53,500
Uruguay	49,015	1027	10,267		(60,309)	44,615	13,210
Venezuela	8740	616			(9,356)	18,920	33,175
Cuba	48,160	45,175			(93,335)	45,631	313,330
Other	87,204	14,784			(101,988)	212,933	390,897
Total	1,177,462	255,032	328,541	164,273	1,925,308	1,300,012	1,457,960

*It is important to note that these figures are not very reliable, although the general magnitude of investment is probably correct.

Sources: W. Woodruff, *Impact of Western Man* (London, 1966) pp. 154–5; Winkler, 1928; Rippy, 1959; Stone, 1968.

accounted for the majority of this (82 per cent in 1920). Railways and related improvements (ports, docks, telegraph, and so on) are generally considered to be necessary and progressive innovations. However, it has been argued that the main result of this development was the reinforcing of export dependence rather than the promotion of broader economic change (see below, pp. 48–9, 65). Other problems were created by the way in which projects were financed. For example, railway and public utility companies and governments which supported these schemes frequently raised money by issuing bonds on which interest was immediately payable. However, it could take a couple of years before the service was operating and able to pay interest. This gap could be bridged only by the continued inflow of new capital. As the burden of foreign debt servicing was often very heavy (for example 35 per cent of export earnings in Argentina 1911–14), this meant that many countries' balance-of-payments position became extremely vulnerable. Perhaps the most dramatic illustration of this problem was the Baring Crisis in Argentina during the 1890s (see below, p. 64). The costs and benefits of foreign borrowing are, however, exceedingly complex issues and can only be properly understood by examining in detail each country's experience.

IMMIGRATION

Marx observed that without abundant supplies of 'free' labour capital cannot reproduce and expand. It is in this sense that an essential concomitant of the massive flow of capital into Latin America was the parallel movement of labour, particularly into sparsely populated Brazil and Argentina. Immigration is usually associated with the very large influx of mainly southern European workers from the last decades of the nineteenth century. But it must be remembered that the 'forced immigration' of black slaves continued to Brazil (until 1850) and Cuba (1865), bringing in over one million slaves from the 1820s. Also, more than 500,000 indentured workers (80 per cent from India) were brought to the British West Indies (1834–1918) to replace slaves, and in Cuba and Peru contracted Chinese were employed in considerable numbers before the trade was ended in 1874. Finally, throughout the century there was a relatively small but fairly steady inflow of European merchants, agricultural colonists, and so on, who settled in virtually all parts, often influencing trade and industry out of all proportion to their numbers. However, in terms of sheer numbers, it was the years from 1880 which were most significant. About 5 million immigrants entered Argentina between 1881 and 1915 and 2.8 million Brazil. Of these about half settled permanently in the two countries. They were attracted to the promise of better opportunities in the New World and pushed by hardship in Europe. Cheap travel and the active recruitment campaigns of labour-hungry Argentines and Brazilians were also important factors. Besides the desire for cheap labour,

> To the Latin American elite in the last quarter of that century, the only road to progress was simply to substitute local manpower by massive immigration or failing to attract it, to hope that a long process of 'whitening' might bleach out racial deficiencies. The vision of progress via immigration was coupled with racial prejudice and racial pessimism . . . .
>
> [Stein and Stein, 1970, *185*]

THE FIRST WORLD WAR AND THE INTERWAR YEARS

Whatever one's views on the costs and benefits of export-led growth, it is beyond question that Latin America was extraordinarily dependent, in the ordinary meaning of the word, on external ties. This dependence and the vulnerability it engendered was dramatically illustrated with the outbreak of the first world war. The 'Guns of August' shattered the delicately balanced structure of the international economy, and the impact on neutral Latin America was immediate and devastating. Shipping was disrupted, banks closed, credit dried up, and consequently commerce ground to a virtual standstill. Governments' incomes (heavily dependent on import duties) were sharply reduced and social tension mounted as food prices rose and unemployment reached alarming levels. After a few months Allied demand for strategic supplies increased and this led to a degree of recovery, but as a result of widespread international dislocation, the war and immediate post-war years remained troubled for most of the republics. Many recent studies of this period have focused on the question of import-substitution, whether the wartime reduction in imports fostered industrial development in the area. If, as most research suggests, it did not [Miller,

1981] this would call into question Frank's key contention that 'The satellites experience their greatest economic development and especially their most classically capitalist industrial development if and when their ties to their metropolis are weakest' [Frank 1969, 9–10], and lend support to the diffusionist view that strong external ties are generally beneficial for development. However, it can be asked if poor wartime industrial performance did not simply indicate the structure weakness of pre-war export-led growth. This and other related questions make the war years a particularly interesting period in which to compare the rival development theories [Albert and Henderson, 1981].

One of the most significant changes hastened by the war was the growth of the United States' economic power in the region. This was already well under way by 1913, the United States dominating trade with Mexico, Central America and most of the Caribbean (including Colombia and Venezuela), and being the single most important market for Brazil and the supplier of imports to Peru. The opening of the Panama Canal in 1914 allowed increased trade with the west coast of South America. By 1927, only in Argentina was the US share of exports less than the British, and then by but a very small margin [Winkler, 1928]. Britain maintained her prewar leadership as a lender, but by 1929 this position too had been substantially eroded by US capital (Table IV). Furthermore, unlike the previous period of investment in infrastructure and government loans, US investors were primarily interested in productive enterprises such as mines, plantations, oil fields, manufacturing, and so on. This marked an important new phase of much greater direct foreign control in Latin America. The strengthened position of the United States here was also part of a more fundamental change in the international economy, namely the emergence in the 1920s of the United States as the world's major creditor nation. However, unlike Britain, the United States was both protectionist and a rather weak importer of primary commodities. This tended to undermine the symbiotic investment–trade relationship between Europe and the periphery, a vital pillar of nineteenth-century economic expansion, by which primary exporters had been able, through a complex network of multilateral settlements, to offset the exchange costs of borrowing by selling to their creditors. An additional difficulty was that wartime shortages had stimulated increased primary commodity production, and from the mid-1920s

Table v

Indicators of Social and Economic Change (Urbanisation, education and railroad mileage in Latin America 1870, 1890, 1910, 1930)

	1870			1890			1910			1930		
	urban.	educa.	rail	urban.	educa.	rail	urban.	educa.	rail	urban.	educa.	rail
Argentina	15.7	–	25	19.3	7.0	168	28.4	9.7	231	38.0	12.6	209
Chile	10.7	–	19	14.8	4.8	63	24.2	11.1	107	32.0	14.2	127
Brazil	6.4	–	8	5.7	2.3	70	9.8	3.0	96	14.0	6.3	97
Colombia	4.5	–	3	5.8	2.3	5	7.3	5.6	13	10.0	7.3	245
Mexico	7.7	–	3	7.4	5.1	48	10.8	5.8	105	15.6	11.1	103
Cuba	–	–	–	–	–	–	28.0	7.1	83	27.3	8.1	79
Peru	6.2	–	10	6.5	2.5	31	5.4	3.5	38	9.6	5.5	47
Venezuela	7.7	–	0	8.4	4.6	11	9.0	1.8	23	19.4	3.7	22
Average	7.8	–	6	9.0	4.7	40	12.9	5.6	61	17.4	8.0	80

(Urbanisation = % of total population in cities of over 20,000; education = % of total population enrolled in schools; railways = .00000 miles per capita. The average figures include data from Bolivia, Costa Rica, Dominican Republic, Ecuador, El Salvador, Guatemala, Honduras, Nicaragua, Panama, Paraguay and Uruguay.)

Sources: D. S. Palmer, *Peru: The Authoritarian Tradition* (New York, 1980) pp. 54–6; Brazil: *O Brazil em numeros* (Rio de Janeiro, 1960).

Table VI*

Indicators of External Dependence 1870–1929 ((1) Main exports as a percentage of total exports. (2) Exports to main foreign market as percentage of total exports. (3) Ratio of total public foreign debt to total export earnings**)

	1870			1888 [1890]			1910 [1914]			1928 [1929]		
	(1)	(2)	(3)	(1)	(2)	(3)	(1)	(2)	(3)	(1)	(2)	(3)
Argentina	45.3	29.2	1.63	39.0	27.7	1.20	42.8	22.9	1.91	23.8	28.7	1.30
Chile	69.8	65.0	.18	83.0	73.5	.71	71.5	26.7	1.45	47.6	34.3	.71
Brazil	46.0	32.0	.77	51.1	–	1.17	41.0	39.5	3.51	71.5	45.4	2.67
Colombia	17.5	64.8	5.31	23.0	29.7	.73	39.5	34.0	1.13	66.0	77.7	.71
Mexico	71.4	70.0	9.78	13.0	73.5	.90	48.7	76.4	1.60	14.7	68.1	2.49
Cuba	–	–	–	–	–	–	56.0	86.8	.61	71.6	72.8	.25
Peru	70.2	81.7	3.88	22.0	37.8	8.67	24.7	38.2	.57	20.9	28.5	.69
Venezuela	43.3	6.8	5.58	72.0	75.5	.69	44.5	35.2	1.00	73.7	35.4	.03
Average:	51.5	44.5	3.82	53.1	47.2	2.59	45.6	52.4	1.43	55.7	53.9	1.12

* These figures and those in Table V are of questionable reliability, although they probably give a reasonable comparative picture.

** For (3) the years are 1870, 1890, 1914 and 1929. The average is constructed in the same manner as in Table v.

Source: same as Table v.

39

ces of these goods began to fall steadily. The faltering interna-
onal economy was finally brought down in ruins by the Crash of
1929. In the 1930s the main supports of externally directed development were significantly undermined. Export earnings, capital
inflows and capacity to import were all sharply reduced. As a
consequence of this in many Latin American countries the years
which followed were to be a time of acute political, social and
economic upheaval leading to, among other things, a fundamental
reassessment of the possibilities of export-led growth.

THE QUESTION OF DEVELOPMENT

The growth of Latin America's links with the international economy
has been outlined, but relatively little has been said about how this
influenced economic development. Reliable data on national income
being unavailable, only a very rough indication of this can be given
(Table v). If development is measured in terms of increasing
urbanisation, education, the growth of exports (Table II) and the
forces of production (transport, productive capacity, and so on)
then many countries experienced a significant degree of progressive
development, particularly from the 1880s. That this was associated
with severe short-term crises, regional economic imbalances, social
dislocation, brutality and oppression does not in essence distinguish
capitalist development here from that in the more advanced countries. What does distinguish it were the particular forms and
excessive degree of external dependence (Table VI) and foreign
control. This situation, encouraged for the most part by local export
elites, helped create structurally inflexible primary-export economies which were extremely vulnerable to outside pressure. Moreover,
whether because of low wages and/or some natural advantage (that
is mineral deposits or vast areas of fertile land), most primary
exports could be produced using relatively primitive techniques.
The imminent necessity to revolutionise continually the forces of
production, possibly the major driving force in metropolitan capitalism, tended therefore to be rather deficient in Latin America.
This meant both a slow transformation of productive structures and
a generally low social productivity of labour. Capitalism in Latin
America was consequently not only dependent, but was also
seriously flawed at its very heart.

In the following sections the historical experiences of four Latin American countries are examined in the light of the general issues raised above. Because much more has been written on Brazil and Argentina than on Chile and Peru the former are accorded fuller treatment. Furthermore, the same questions are not pursued in each study, for what is being presented is not a summary analysis of these countries' external economic relations, but primarily a survey of the principal debates concerning these relations.

3 Brazil

BRAZIL, discovered by the Portuguese around 1500, did not afford the easy plunder or the readily exploitable mines and labour that the Spanish found in New Spain (Mexico) and Peru. To secure this vast territory (about one-half of the continent) they therefore brought in African slaves to cultivate sugar cane, a combination which had proved successful in their Atlantic islands. During three centuries of colonial rule there were many important changes – the gradual decline of sugar from the late seventeenth century, the diamond and gold boom (1690–1770) centred in Minas Gerais, and the steady growth of cattle-raising in the interior of the north-east – but slavery, large landholdings and the export of primary products remained dominant. They were carried over into the nineteenth century as the prime features of the country's colonial heritage.

It is this colonial heritage which many writers regard as a central factor in explaining the course of Brazil's subsequent history. Run as a plantation economy by the Portuguese, the country was in fact commercially dominated first by the Dutch, who controlled much of the colony's shipping as well as the sugar and slave trades, and later by the British, protectors of the weak Portuguese throne. Frank [1969, *151*] has accordingly argued that Brazil was created and actively underdeveloped as part of the expansion of commercial capitalism from the sixteenth century onwards. He writes, 'what the capitalist metropolis did implant in Brazil was not an archaic economic and social structure but rather the still alive and developing metropolis-satellite structure of capitalism itself.' While it is obviously correct to draw attention to the context within which Brazil's colonial economy was formed, it is somewhat more problematic to label the result 'capitalism'. As Laclau [1971] observes, by defining capitalism as essentially production for profit and the market and ignoring the question of forces and relations of production, Frank's construct is so broad as to be meaningless. For Marxist theoreticians, such as Laclau, this represents a major flaw in the dependency formulation. This debate is also of wider interest in that it closely parallels the long-running controversy among Marxist scholars about the transition from feudalism to capitalism in Europe.[7]

Independence (1822) did not mean Brazil was free to pursue her economic destiny unfettered by outside forces. The colonial social and economic structures which had tied her so closely to Europe remained intact and the state remained firmly in the hands of the rural oligarchy. This helped ensure the continuance of both export-dependence and slavery. In the 1820s one-third to one-half of Brazil's population of about four million were slaves, and a great many more were brought in by mid-century. Slavery itself was not finally abolished until 1888. An important feature of Brazil's continued external domination were the substantial concessions exacted by the British [Manchester, 1933]. In return for official recognition, a diplomatic and economic necessity, Brazil signed treaties (1826 and 1827) agreeing to end the slave trade by 1830 and granting special privileges to British trade, most importantly a maximum 15 per cent *ad valorem* import duty. These treaties, extensions of similar ones forced upon the Portuguese during the court's British-sponsored exile in Rio, had contradictory effects. By making it difficult to protect local production against cheaper imports they tended to reinforce Brazil's export role. At the same time by attacking slavery the treaty of 1826 threatened the very basis of the export economy. However, because of the overriding importance of slavery, Brazilian efforts to stop the trade were no more than half-hearted. During the ensuing twenty-five years Britain had continually to harass the government both diplomatically and by the use of naval force before the slave trade was finally ended about 1850.

These aspects of Brazil's independence have been the subject of some controversy. While it is generally agreed that Brazil was coerced by Britain, the effects of this coercion with respect to trade are in dispute. Frank and the Steins have argued that the unequal trade treaty of 1827, which was in force for fifteen years, made it impossible for Brazil to protect her industry and forced her to continue as an exporter of primary products [Frank, 1969; Stein and Stein, 1970]. Furtado [1963], on the other hand, contends that although the limitation on the level of import duties seriously compromised the government's financial position, export-led growth was the only practical option given the economy's overall structure and orientation. 'Hence', he writes, 'there are no grounds for thinking that if the Brazilian government had enjoyed full liberty to act, the country's economic development would have been more rapid' [*103*]. His case is persuasive, for there was at best an extremely weak basis for domestically induced growth. The British were merely pushing the economy in a direction to which it was already overwhelmingly committed.

The slave-trade issue has also been vigorously debated. Calogeras argues that by wounding Brazilian pride, British anti-slave trade policies actually gave a boost to the traffic, this being demonstrated by the substantial increase in the trade following the passage of the Aberdeen Act of 1845 which authorised more forceful direct action against slavers. Echoing the claims of the Brazilian government of the day, Calogeras writes:[8] 'When it came to final and definite suppression . . . the drastic measures adopted by Brazil in 1850 owed nothing either in their elaboration or enforcement to Great Britain. The efforts were Brazil's and to Brazil belongs the credit.' This view does not, however, stand up to a detailed analysis of documentary sources, such as that undertaken by Bethell [1970]. He comments,

> It is clear . . . that it was the sudden extension in June and July [1850] of the British squadron's anti-slavery trade operations into Brazilian inland waters and ports which by provoking a major political crisis in Brazil, led directly to the passage of a new anti-slave trade law and to its vigorous enforcement. [*363*]

It must be stressed that this is but one of the many important questions raised by an international political struggle which lasted for more than two decades [Manchester, 1933; Graham, 1968].

THE GROWTH OF COFFEE EXPORTS

Although Brazil's exports – sugar, cotton, tobacco, hides, and so on – prospered during the Napoleonic Wars, from the 1820s earnings stagnated as prices fell and the terms of trade became unfavourable. Sugar, the principal commodity, faced strong competition in the world market, and exports rose slowly. Furtado [1963] argues that 'The main cause of the great relative backwardness of the Brazilian economy in the first half of the nineteenth century was . . . the damming up of exports' [*116*]. The dam was to be broken by coffee.

Table VII
Coffee Exports 1820–1930 (Thousands of 60-kg bags)

Year	Exports	% of country's total exports	% of world coffee production
1820	129	–	–
1840/1	1195	(1843) 59	–
1860	3115	53	56
1880	5783	63	58
1900	11,285	(1901) 60	75
1913	14,547	62	74
1930	15,519	63	65

Sources: Holloway, 1980; W. Baer, *Industrialisation and Economic Development in Brazil* (Homewood, Illinois, 1965) pp. 274–7.

Coffee had been grown for local consumption in Brazil from the early eighteenth century, but it was only from about the 1820s that commercial production, stimulated by rising world prices, began in earnest. This took place first in the hinterland of Rio de Janeiro, where fertile, virgin soil and slave labour were combined on large plantations (*fazendas*) in the Paraíba Valley to produce a rapid spread of coffee cultivation. Exports rose substantially in the first decades of the century (Table VII), and by the late 1830s coffee had outstripped sugar in importance, Brazil soon becoming the world's single largest coffee producer. In the 1870s and 1880s growers in the Rio area began to suffer from a combination of soil exhaustion, labour scarcity, declining productivity and mounting debts. At about this time coffee production was expanding rapidly in the western part of São Paulo. By the mid-1890s exports from the port of Santos surpassed those from Rio, and by the first world war were almost three times as great. Virtually the entire increase in coffee production from the 1880s to 1930 came from the São Paulo region.

The success of coffee-growing in São Paulo was based on the availability of vast areas of extremely fertile land and, until 1888, slave labour. Rapid expansion was stimulated both by more than a decade of rising world coffee prices from 1885 and by the devaluation of the *milreis* after 1890. It also owed a great deal to foreign capital and immigrant labour, neither of which had had a significant impact during the early period of expansion around Rio, although foreign merchants had achieved a dominant position here.

FOREIGN INVESTMENT

It is undeniable that foreign capital played a major part in the growth of Brazil's export economy, but in the process serious problems were generated. From the latter decades of the nineteenth century the level of foreign investment increased rapidly (Table VIII), government loans taking the largest single share (Tables VIII and IX). The servicing of this debt put a heavy charge on the country's balance of payments. It is estimated [Villela and Suzigan, 1977] that during the empire (1822–89) one-and-a-half times the entire period's balance of trade surplus was required to cover the government's foreign obligations. In the years 1890–1933 this fell to 75 per cent, but at the same time the total debt rose by almost nine times. The government frequently had to borrow in order to meet its payments on existing loans. Therefore when coffee prices fell and/or the inflow of funds dried up, financial and economic crisis ensued; funding or rescheduling loans had to be negotiated (1898, 1914, 1931). Thus the debt mounted. Further problems were created by exchange depreciation, which was particularly marked for almost a decade from 1890 and again in the early and late 1920s. Although a declining *milreis* benefited exporters by increasing their income in local currency, and industrialists by raising the price of competing imports, it put greater pressure on the state, which had to service its external debt with foreign currency. This and the increasing debt had a number of effects. The substantial fixed interest charges increased the vulnerability of an economy which because of its dependence on coffee exports was already extremely susceptible to external disequilibrium. Secondly, the need to renegotiate the debt meant that the country's fiscal and monetary policies were often dictated by its foreign creditors. This generally involved deflationary measures which created considerable hardship for Brazil's structurally rather inflexible economy (see below, p. 55). For example, in 1898 foreign bankers demanded that the government withdraw a substantial quantity of paper money from circulation and refrain from contracting new loans for three years.

Table VIII

Accumulated Foreign Investment in Brazil 1865–1927 (£000, and Share of Government Loans

	Britain	US	France	Germany	% in government securities
1865	20,284	–	–	–	64
1875	30,928	–	–	–	66
1885	47,641	–	–	–	49
1895	92,988	–	–	–	56
1905	122,903	–	–	–	68
1913	254,812	10,267	143,737	102,670	47 (GB)
1927	280,065	70,311	11,024	–	53

Sources: Stone, 1968; W. Woodruff, *Impact of Western Man* (London, 1966) pp. 154–5; Winkler, 1928.

Table IX

Unrepaid Debt of Brazilian Government 1855–1927 –Federal, State and Municipal (£000)

1855	3,576
1865	14,320
1875	18,024
1885	10,510
1895	39,817
1905	79,043
1913	145,252
1927	235,206

Source: *O Brazil em numeros* (Rio de Janeiro, 1960) pp. 145–6.

Finally, excessive borrowing made it necessary to find new loans simply to finance interest and repayment. This gives credence to Villela and Suzigan's argument that 'Liberal borrowing abroad undermined any rational policy to use external credit for purposes of economic development' [269].

RAILWAYS

Railways in Brazil absorbed the largest single proportion of foreign capital. It is, however, impossible to provide exact figures, for besides foreign ownership of some lines and loans to Brazilian companies, much federal and state borrowing went to finance rail-building. As early as 1835, legislation provided for concessions for railway-construction, but it was not until 5 per cent interest guarantees were offered in 1852 that the first line was built (on a section of the route between Rio and Petropolis). This was a Brazilian venture. So too was the second line (the Dom Pedro Segundo) through the Paraíba Valley. Foreign investors only became interested in these and similar projects once local entrepreneurs had demonstrated their potential. Expansion was fairly modest during the next two decades (Table x), but from the 1870s the rate of growth picked up considerably, stimulated not only by high export earnings, but also by higher interest guarantees (7 per cent) and the offer of favourable exchange rates for the remission abroad of dividends. In Brazil, although 80 per cent of the lines were privately managed and some of the most important and profitable companies were in British hands, none the less by the first world war the government was the principal owner of railways (61 per cent). By this time similar degrees of state ownership were found in Chile (56 per cent) and Mexico (70 per cent).

The railway came to the Paraíba Valley after coffee production was at its peak [Stein, 1957], while expansion of the more extensive coffee frontier in São Paulo was almost totally dependent on the growth of the rail network. This was because of the great distances involved and the fact that transport was such a large part of total costs. For example, even with the railways, 20 per cent of coffee income was spent on transport to Santos in the 1920s [Coes, 1970]. Clearly then, railways were a crucial factor in opening up Brazil. But at what cost? It has been argued that because lines were built essentially to connect areas of export production to the ports no national system was established and the wider impact of the railways was therefore limited. Mattoon [1977] contends that although the potential for economic and social transformation was

48

Table x
Railway Development in Brazil 1854–1930

km of track in operation in the year ending:

1854	15	1900	15,316
1860	223	1910	21,326
1870	745	1920	28,535
1880	3398	1930	32,478
1890	9973		

Sources: L. Randall, *A Comparative Economic History of Latin America 1500–1914*, vol. iii: Brazil (Ann Arbor, Mich., 1977) p. 233; *O Brazil em numeros*, p. 61.

great, in São Paulo, where the rail system was the most fully developed, this potential was never realised. The railways tended to strengthen the traditional plantation system and did not provide a market for locally produced manufactured goods. However, looking at the question of the distribution of goods, Dean [1969] claims that by extending the local market the railways made an important contribution to domestic industrial development. Another issue is the financing of the railways. Villela and Suzigan [1977] maintain that because of government guarantees, the lines were more expensive to build than they might have been. Difficulties of measurement make this an impossible question to resolve, but it is apparent that the massive debt contracted in order to build the railways did impose a severe burden on the government and the economy.

IMMIGRATION

The other major external contribution to Brazil's economic growth, besides capital and technology, was European labour. Successful agricultural settlements were established from the early decades of the century by German and Swiss colonists in the southern states of Rio Grande do Sol and Santa Catarina, but these provided no labour for the coffee estates. Initial attempts to do this failed in the 1840s and 1850s, largely because of the lack of organisation and the appalling conditions associated with slavery. These conditions and the high ratio of male to female slaves meant that the continued importation of slaves was necessary to prevent a decline in the captive labour force. Therefore, after the trade ended in 1850 the price of slaves rose, and the system itself began a slow but irreversible decline. As more planters became aware of this concerted efforts were made, especially from the 1870s, to attract workers from Europe. The results were not, however, very encouraging until the mid- to late 1880s (Table XI) when it became fairly clear that slavery would soon be abolished. But abolition was resisted by the São Paulo planters until almost the very end. Their resistance was finally overcome, according to Conrad [1972] primarily by the flight of slaves from the *fazendas*, rather than as Holloway [1980] has argued by the alternative labour supply afforded by the influx of immigrants. However, as both events coincided, it is somewhat difficult to distinguish their relative impact on abolition.

There were substantial variations in the immigrant flow over time. This was in response to conditions in southern Europe, where most of the immigrants came from, and to the changing economic situation in Brazil. It is interesting to note that most immigrants went to the state of São Paulo drawn by the coffee estates, and that in the period of 1889–1900 about 80 per cent of the new arrivals were subsidised by the government. Finally, while the foreign-born comprised only about 7 per cent of the country's population, in rural São Paulo 56 per cent of the agricultural workers in 1905 were foreigners [Holloway, 1980, *63*]. Immigration was an essential concomitant of the development of São Paulo's coffee industry in the post-slavery years. None the less, Leff [1973] has argued that for the Brazilian economy as a whole the effects of large-scale immigration were negative. The elastic supply of labour it afforded both held down real wages and forestalled the movement of labour from the 'backward' subsistence sector to the modern export sector. This in turn contributed to the slow transformation of the country's socio-economic structure. Although provocative, this argument tends to ignore the many difficulties faced by the planters both in recruiting local labour, many of whom preferred subsistence agriculture to the harsh plantation regimes, and in holding on to immigrant workers.

Table xi
Immigration into Brazil 1858–1940

Gross immigration				Net immigration	
1858–67	123,898	1898–1907	578,253	1872–90	570,266
1868–77	169,530	1908–17	934,269	1891–1900	903,454
1878–87	298,631	1918–27	630,178	1901–20	939,953
1888–97	1,265,090	1928–37	465,026	1920–40	859,842

Source: *O Brazil em numeros*, pp. 11–12.

THE COFFEE ECONOMY

Brazil exported a great variety of products including cotton, sugar, tobacco, hides, cocoa, but except for the relatively short-lived Amazonian rubber boom (from the 1880s to the first world war), the dominance of coffee was unrivalled (see Table vii). The earnings of this sector, even though concentrated in the coffee-producing states, determined the prosperity of the entire economy. It is therefore necessary to say something about the particular characteristics of the production and marketing of coffee as these had an important bearing on the course of the country's development.

The coffee plant takes from four to six years to bear fruit, reaches peak output between six and eight years and can go on producing for another three to four decades. It was, therefore, virtually impossible for the industry to respond in the short, or even medium, term to price changes. Moreover, because virgin land was relatively so abundant, even if the price of coffee was low it could pay growers to increase plantings simply to hold on to their workers, much of whose livelihood came from planting food crops between the rows of coffee seedlings. 'In this way,' writes Holloway, 'coffee expansion became a device for retaining the labor force, rather than as a response to favorable coffee prices' [1980, *88*]. It also contributed to an inbuilt tendency for overproduction in the long run. The year-to-year picture was, however, rather different. Because of the coffee plant's extreme sensitivity to frost and to substantial variations in yield, output tends to vary quite markedly from one year to the next, resulting in either glut or scarcity on the world market. At the same time, the demand for coffee tended to be relatively inelastic, the quantity sold not varying significantly with changes in prices. These factors combined to make the profitability of coffee production extremely uncertain. To make matters worse, planters had little access to long-term loans and therefore became heavily indebted, especially in bad years, to export merchants and other middlemen. Inadequate storage facilities added to the growers' difficulties, making it impossible for them to hold stocks against price rises. For these and other reasons planters were in a weak position *vis-à-vis* the merchants. Finally, the fact that the export trade was dominated by a few large foreign firms – between 1895 and 1906 over 70 per cent of Santos's coffee was shipped by ten houses – made the planter–merchant relationship a particularly sensitive issue and led to accusations that foreign merchants and speculators manipulated the market to their own advantage. This was no doubt true, but the extent of this type of collusion and the effects it had on the planters and the Brazilian economy remain open questions [Holloway, 1975; Greenhill, 1977].

These problems were more or less obscured until the mid-1890s by steadily rising coffee prices and a depreciating exchange rate. These favourable conditions together with a high rate of domestic inflation from the early 1890s meant high profits for the planters and occasioned a dramatic increase in planting. For example, between 1886 and 1900 the number of coffee trees in São Paulo rose from 154,292,000 to 571,614,000 [Holloway, 1980, *178*], while the country's coffee production almost doubled. From the late 1890s overproduction and falling prices had become chronic problems. The bumper harvest of 1906, twice the size of the previous year's, finally provoked action from the planters. Representatives from the three major coffee-growing states of Rio de Janeiro, São Paulo and Minas Gerais met at Taubate, in the state of São Paulo, to devise a plan for stabilising prices by taking excess stocks off the market. This novel procedure, known as valorisation, was in the end put into practice by São Paulo alone. It proved successful in supporting coffee prices, but in the process new problems were created. Villela and Suzigan [1977] argue that valorisation interfered with the operation of the market, thereby leading to the misallocation of investment, the retardation of other sectors, and the lack of agricultural diversification. 'It is true', they write, 'that industry and transportation benefited from the periodic rise in the terms of trade and the capacity to import. But the question remains as to whether the Brazilian economy might not have grown and diversified more rapidly had there been no coffee-support program' [16]. It would seem enough to assess the cause and consequences of valorisation without pursuing such chimerical propositions. Secondly, although valorisation was intended to protect planters from the vagaries of the market and the machinations of foreign merchants, the scheme could only be carried out with the close co-operation of those very merchants together with foreign bankers. Moreover, the loans raised to finance valorisation increased the country's external debt and gave foreign interests greater influence over economic policy. Finally, stable prices gave a boost to coffee production both in other parts of the world and, because there was no control over new planting, in Brazil itself. The consequent increase in output made it necessary to reintroduce valorisation in 1917, 1922 and regularly from 1925. It would seem that the attempt to manage the world market weakened Brazil's hold on that market, while at the same time tying the country more firmly to it.

CONCLUSIONS

Having identified and discussed various aspects of Brazil's links with the international economy, it is time to turn to the key question of how these links influenced the course of economic change. Did participation in the world economy foster progressive change or simply reinforce the 'colonial heritage'? Was there modernisation or an intensification of structural underdevelopment? A preliminary, and very rough, answer can be given by referring to the data in Tables V and VI. In comparison with other Latin American countries it appears that Brazil's 'development' was more or less average, but the extent of external dependence was considerably above average. The point at issue is the exact nature of this development and the weight to be given to the various problems associated with it.

Furtado [1963] estimates that in the second half of the nineteenth century per-capita income in Brazil rose by 2.3 per cent per year in the coffee states and 1.5 per cent in the country as a whole. At the same time, population grew (from 7.3 to 18 million), urban areas developed, and the country's commercial and transport infrastructures underwent radical transformation. Such evidence of growth and change has led Coes [1970] to conclude that the years 1880–1913 were a time of considerable prosperity for Brazil, and

53

Graham [1968] to argue that by the first world war the nation was launched on a 'modernizing trajectory'. Neither author completely ignores the serious difficulties such as the economic stagnation and extreme poverty of the north-east (37 per cent of population in 1920) or the excessive degree of external dependence, which remained unresolved. They tend, however, to give less emphasis to these and similar problems in their final assessments. Another optimistic argument is offered by Peláez [1976]. He maintains that in the period 1857–1906 Brazil enjoyed a considerable improvement in her income terms of trade, which together with sound monetary policy permitted stable economic growth and modernisation. Furtado [1963], on the other hand, claims that despite the rapid rate of economic growth, because of her relative late integration into the modern world economy, Brazil's backwardness was not overcome by the early decades of the twentieth century. Leff [1973] accepts the last point but judges the causes to have been rather different. Pointing out that the slow growth of exports from the north and north-east reduced the impact of coffee earnings on the entire Brazilian economy, he maintains that 'the effects of trade in promoting Brazilian economic development were limited not by colonialism or deteriorating terms of trade, but by the low overall export growth, the small share of the export sector in the economy [i.e. a large subsistence sector], and the elastic supply of labour' [*692*]. This challenging analysis can be faulted in that Leff pays little attention to the problems created by either the large external debt, the structure of coffee production and marketing, or foreign economic control. But, by claiming that there was a need for more extensive export development, he provides a clear alternative to the dependency argument which generally equates the growth of primary exports with underdevelopment. More summary views on Brazilian economic development could be given, but it is more useful to end this section by narrowing the perspective somewhat.

The chief feature of Brazil's economic transformation was the growth of coffee exports. However, from the 1890s an industrial sector, given over mainly to the production of basic consumer goods, also began to grow with some rapidity. Although the reasons for this are debated, both exchange depreciation and tariffs were instrumental [Versiani, 1979]. Because industry is widely, and often uncritically, used as a proxy for development, various aspects of Brazilian industrialisation have become the focus of controversy.

One of these is the impact of the first world war. Frank [1969], basing his analysis on the work of Normano and Simonson, maintains that when links with the metropolis were weakened during the first world war industrial growth was stimulated in São Paulo. For him this demonstrates the drag imposed on development by the combination of export and import dependence and vindicates his general thesis. This argument on wartime industrialisation has been strongly, and on the whole convincingly, challenged on empirical grounds by a number of scholars including Leff [1973], Dean [1969], Villela and Suzigan [1977] and Peláez [1977]. While they each stress different factors, the basic argument is that reduced coffee exports led to decreases in real incomes, effective demand and the capacity to import. Due to the latter, and the difficulty of obtaining capital goods and raw materials during the war, industry was unable to expand its plant. Increased industrial output came from a more intensive use of existing capacity. Dean [1969] comments, 'It might be asked if the industrialisation of São Paulo would not have proceeded faster had there been no war' [104]. Even if this argument were correct [see Fishlow, 1972] and industry flourished only when coffee exports were buoyant, given the many problems associated with this crop it was surely not a sound basis for industrial development. The lack of significant industrial growth during the war partially reflects this and in doing so highlights the fundamental brittleness of Brazil's coffee-based development.

COLONY AND INDEPENDENCE

THROUGHOUT most of the colonial period the Rio de la Plata area, from which Argentina was to be formed, was a backwater of the Spanish empire. The most important centres of economic activity were located in the interior provinces of the north-west and the northern littoral from which food, livestock and other goods were supplied to the mines of Upper Peru. Buenos Aires and the coast were linked somewhat hazardously to this region through a countryside dominated by nomadic, often hostile, Indian tribes. External trade from Buenos Aires was restricted, Lima being the official entrepot, but by the eighteenth century contraband, particularly in silver, had assumed substantial importance. In an effort to control the trade and to counter the military threat to this exposed flank of the empire, the Spanish set up the Viceroyalty of Rio de la Plata in 1776. This included not only Argentina, but also parts of what were to become Bolivia, Paraguay and Uruguay. The opening of trade through Buenos Aires gave a tremendous stimulus to the coastal economy, merchants prospered, and the city's population grew from 12,000 in 1750 to 50,000 by the end of the century. Pastoral production such as hides, tallow and salted meat increased and the port gained control of the trade in precious metals which accounted for about 80 per cent of the region's exports in the 1790s. This period marked the beginning of a fundamental shift in the balance of economic power between the coast and the interior as mining declined and trade across the Atlantic became more important.

In the Rio de la Plata the break with Spain came earlier and was achieved more easily than in other parts of the empire. Spanish power was weaker here, as was dramatically shown in 1806 and again in 1807 when the authorities proved unable to defend Buenos Aires against the landing of British troops. On both occasions it was local, mainly creole, volunteers who finally repelled the invaders. British troops were clearly unwelcome, but not British trade. The desire of the creole merchants for freer trade, encouraged by the relaxation of commercial controls during the Napoleonic wars, had a major influence on Buenos Aires' successful bid for independence in 1810 following the fall of the Spanish monarchy. National independence was not officially declared until 1816. After this there ensued a long period of political turmoil as regional interests battled either for complete autonomy (quickly achieved by Bolivia and Paraguay, and only in 1830 by Uruguay) or over the structure of the new state, rather inappropriately called the 'United Provinces'.

THE POST-INDEPENDENCE YEARS: 1830–80

The violent political struggles which occurred in the decades after independence were essentially concerned with the questions of whether there should be a centralised or loosely federated state, what policies to adopt on landholding and foreign trade, and which group should control the customs revenue collected at the port of Buenos Aires. The *unitarios*, the military, merchants and intellectuals from the port city, whose most prominent spokesman was Rivadavia, wanted a strong 'liberal' regime, encouragement for small farmers, free trade and the development of the country on what they perceived to be the European model. However, they were able to hold power for only a short time in the 1820s. It was the *federales* from the province of Buenos Aires, led by Juan Manuel de Rosas, who emerged victorious by the early 1830s. They supported regional self-determination and the interests of the large landholding cattle-raisers. It is often argued that because the Buenos Aires federalists monopolised customs receipts and favoured the growth of an export economy, they contributed to the economic decline of the interior provinces. Burgin [1946] contends that this conflict between a confident externally directed coast and a defensive protectionist interior was at the heart of four decades of civil war. This view, as it related to economic conditions in the interior, has been challenged by Brown [1979]. He maintains that the growth of Buenos Aires' foreign trade provided improved market opportunities for products from the interior, and that it was mainly inadequate transport facilities which prevented dynamic development in the more distant provinces. This argument needs to be substantiated in greater detail.

Rosas was overthrown in 1852, a decade later provincial unity was established by Mitre, and national unification was finally achieved in 1880 when Buenos Aires became the Argentine capital. During this long period the foundations were laid for the country's subsequent export boom. Under the 1853 Constitution of the

Argentine Confederation immigration was actively promoted for the first time since Rivadavia's efforts in the 1820s. The attitude of the ruling elite was summed up in Juan B. Alberdi's famous dictum of the time, 'To govern is to populate.' Despite continued civil unrest, in these years over 400,000 immigrants entered the country. To give some idea of the relative importance of this influx, at the first census in 1869 there were but 1,800,000 people in the entire country. In 1857, the first rail line was completed, running ten kilometres from Buenos Aires, and by 1880 almost 2560 kilomètres of track had been added. With this came a resurgence of foreign borrowing, which had been at a virtual standstill since the defaults of the 1820s. Stone estimates that between 1865 and 1875 British investment in government loans and railways increased by £18.8 million, giving Argentina in the latter year a much higher level of British capital per inhabitant (£10) than either Mexico (£2.8) or Brazil (£2.5). Only profligate, guano-rich Peru could boast a larger figure (£13) (see Table I). These years also witnessed a substantial expansion in Argentina's exports, composed mainly of skins and hides, wool, tallow, and salted beef. The total value of exports rose from around £2 million in the 1850s to over £11 million by 1880.

Against the widely held view that Argentine development in these years was spurred on by external factors, Platt [1980] argues that domestic needs were of primary importance in explaining growth, particularly the need to provision the rapidly expanding Buenos Aires market. This novel position finds qualified support from Lewis [forthcoming] who maintains that, although the influence of the export sector was important, in looking for the motives behind early railway development equal weight should be accorded to local demand and the political necessity of national integration. It is reasonable to point out that domestic concerns had an influence on railway construction and Argentine development generally, but in neither case has much hard evidence yet been adduced which casts serious doubt on the many scholarly studies which have stressed the primacy in this period of external stimuli [Goodwin, 1977; Brown, 1979; Reber, 1979; Stein and Stein, 1980].

1880–1930

Relative domestic political stability, improved ocean and inland transport, increased foreign demand for Argentine products, mounting inflows of labour and capital, the final genocidal assault on the pampas Indians (1879–81) and the expansion of the agricultural frontier which this made possible were some of the more important factors underlying a sustained period of export-led growth which lasted, with substantial fluctuations, until the international economy upon which it was based collapsed in 1929. Diaz-Alejandro writes [1970, *3*],

> From 1860 to 1930 Argentina grew at a rate that has few parallels in economic history, perhaps comparable only to the performance during the same years of other countries of recent settlement ... the fifty years before 1914 witnessed one of the highest growth rates in the world for such a prolonged period of time.

Taking up this theme, Cortés Conde [1974, *152*] adds that by the first world war

> The entire country had changed, not only the rural landscape where desert had given way to seas of wheat and trees and dwellings, revealing the presence of humans in formerly empty landscape, but cities, where poor, austere structures ... were replaced by a style which mirrored the new wealth and strove to repeat the style of the great European metropolises.

The figures in Table XII suggest that the development was indeed impressive. However, as will be seen, many historians claim that because of the particular political and economic formations upon which this development depended and the nature of the external links and obligations which made it possible, the dramatic rates of growth cannot be equated with the progressive transformation of the Argentine economy.

THE EXPORT SECTORS

Over the entire period there was a spectacular growth in the volume and value of exports and important changes in both product composition (Table XIII) and the organisation of production. A strong demand for coarse wool and tallow from Europe and good grazing for sheep on land near the city of Buenos Aires combined to make wool the first of Argentina's 'modern' export sectors. It

Table XII

Some Indicators of Argentinian Growth 1865–1929

	Population	Railways (km)	Exports (million gold pesos)	Imports (million gold pesos)	Area in crops (million hectares)	Quantum of exports	Quantum of imports
1865–9	1,709,000	503	29.6	38.0	.58 (1872)	–	–
1880–4	2,680,000	3000	62.0	73.0	2.46 (1888)	–	–
1910–14	7,200,000	31,000	402.0	359.0	20.62	100	100
1925–9	10,970,000	38,435	–	–	25.18	176.6	143.6

Sources:Ford, 1975, p. 14; Diaz-Alejandro, 1970, pp. 2, 151.

Table XIII

Argentine Exports: Quantity (annual average) and Percentage of Total Export Value 1880–1929

	1880–4 tons	% of value	1910–14 tons	% of value	1925–9 tons	% of value
Wool	109,000	58	137,000	12.9	136,000	8.2
Hides & skins	70,000	32	125,000	11.0	181,000	8.1
Wheat	34,000	1.6	2,118,000	19.4	4,233,000	22.2
Maize	56,000	1.8	3,194,000	17.9	5,521,000	18.5
Linseed	18,000	1.7	679,000	10.2	1,618,000	12.2
Frozen beef	–	–	304,000	7.6	201,000	3.3
Chilled beef	–	–	25,000	0.6	402,000	7.5

Source: Diaz-Alejandro, 1970, pp. 5, 18, 474.

began to be established on a systematic basis in the 1850s and by the 1880s was providing between 50 and 60 per cent of the country's export earnings. Scobie [1964, *Argentina, 86*] notes how 'Sheep attracted immigrants and capital, encouraged the conquest and settlement of the pampas and provided a favorable environment for breeding, crops, railroads and packing – in a word, conditions necessary for Argentine wheat and beef supremacy in the twentieth century.'

The second phase of export expansion was led by wheat and other cereal crops. The former was first grown in the 1860s by farmers and agricultural colonists in the provinces of Santa Fe and Entre Rios to meet domestic demand. As the railway network was extended and surpluses increased, so exports became more important, particularly from the 1890s. The area of land under wheat rose from 73,000 hectares in 1872 to 1,202,000 by 1890 and to almost 7,000,000 by the first world war [Di Tella and Zymelman, 1967, *39*]. Over these years the centre of production shifted to the province of Buenos Aires. This entailed significant changes in productive organisation for here large landholdings were dominant and cereals were grown by short-term tenants, not owner–occupiers. Gallo [1977] has argued that the latter system, as found in Santa Fe, led to a significant degree of social differentiation and progressive change in that region. Scobie [1964, *Revolution*] in his study of tenant-based production in Buenos Aires points out that here the concentration of landholding meant immigrant tenants and harvest workers remained impoverished, as did the countryside generally, because the profits from wheat were accumulated by absentee landowners in the city of Buenos Aires. This afforded inordinate economic and political power to the landowning oligarchy and according to some writers (see below, p. 68) this was a major barrier to progressive change in Argentina. The contrast between the organisation of wheat-growing in Buenos Aires province and the northern littoral demonstrates the importance of the form of the productive structure in determining the wider impact of export growth.

Wheat-growing tenants cleared the land, planted their crops for a few years and then were moved on, having to leave the land in alfalfa for the owner's cattle. In this way wheat cultivation prepared the pampas for the modern cattle industry, which expanded rapidly from the late nineteenth century. Improved breeds were introduced, refrigerated shipping was made more efficient, and a meat-packing industry sprang up to channel Argentine beef to foreign markets, Britain being by far the most important of these. It was meat-packing, controlled by a few very large British and US companies, which became a major focus for claims that foreign imperialists dominated and manipulated the Argentine economy. The packers did exercise enormous power through price fixing, market sharing and shipping pools, but Greenhill and Crossley [1977] argue that such factors as inter-company disputes, changing market and supply conditions and outside competition imposed constraints on their ability to control the beef trade. Foreign packers, nevertheless, wielded very considerable influence in Argentina, as shown during the crisis of the post-war years when they were able to defeat all attempts by the state to regulate their activities [Smith, 1969]. It is entirely understandable, especially when times were hard, that these firms should have become the objects of suspicion and resentment.

FOREIGN INVESTMENT

The flow of foreign capital into Argentina, mainly from Britain, grew spectacularly from the mid-1880s, Argentina being touted as another United States. An investment mania ensued with British holdings rising from about £20 million in 1880 to £160 million ten years later. By 1890 debt servicing absorbed about 60 per cent of the country's export earnings. Because a high proportion of this debt was in the form of fixed interest securities (usually quoted in foreign currency) on projects such as railways which required a considerable time before they could stimulate increased production and exports, a continued inflow of new loans was essential to maintain the balance of payments position. Furthermore, as in Brazil, a falling exchange rate, pronounced in Argentina from the late 1880s to 1899, made repayment more onerous. For example, the depreciation of the peso between 1888 and 1891 effectively increased the sterling debt by 160 per cent. But this was only for sterling loans, and in Argentina a great deal of foreign borrowing by landowners had been carried out by means of land mortgage bonds (cédulas) repayable in local currency. For this large and politically influential group of debtors, as well as exporters generally and many industrialists, devaluation was a blessing.

However, by 1889 investor's enthusiasm started to wane because of fears about Argentina's heavy debt burden and her economic prospects. Loans dried up and a major financial panic, the Baring Crisis, followed. It was not until 1905 that the interest of foreign investors revived. In this second boom, capital from France, Germany and the United States assumed greater importance, Britain's share falling from 80 per cent at the turn of the century to 60 per cent by 1913. In the post-war years US investment continued to increase, marking the onset of this country's more aggressive economic interest in Argentina.

It is extremely difficult to assess the impact of foreign lending on Argentina, not only because the issue is complex in itself, but also because it was bound up inseparably with the entire process of export-led development. Obviously, foreign capital was instrumental in the formation of much of the country's transport and municipal infrastructure (that is gas works, water and power companies), but as in the case of Brazil, it also engendered increased economic vulnerability. This was shown dramatically by the Baring Crisis, the effects of which, in terms of a fall-off in immigration, rail-building and the level of economic activity generally, were felt for many years. For example, the value of exports and imports did not reach their 1889 level until 1898 and 1904 respectively. Besides the continual problem posed to the balance of payments position by heavy debt-servicing obligations, other difficulties arose because the level of income in Argentina came to be dependent on inflows of foreign capital and export earnings [Ford, 1962]. These in turn were determined by economic conditions in the metropolitan countries, particularly Britain, where when conditions deteriorated it was possible to protect the balance of payments by raising the Bank Rate thereby reducing the level of both overseas lending and the demand for imports. However, Argentina was powerless to defend herself against such adjustments because foreign capital and exports comprised the very life blood of the economy. Factors such as this, together with the leading, if not dominant, role of the British in commerce, banking, export processing, shipping and railways are a measure of the degree of informal imperialist control to which Argentina was subjected. To claim, as Ferns [1960, 488] does, that such control did not exist because 'The British Government has never had the power to oblige Argentina to pay a debt, to pay a dividend, or to export or import any commodity whatsoever,' is at best irrelevant.

RAILWAYS

Just as in Brazil, railways in Argentina came to account for the largest single share of foreign capital (about 60 per cent of British investment in 1913). A striking difference was the extent of foreign ownership (Table XIV), making the railways, together with the packing plants, a legitimate target for nationalists' accusations of foreign domination. The debate on the effect of the railroads is similar to that over export-led growth (see below, pp. 67-8). For example, Scobie [1964, *Revolution*] suggests that the railways afforded few wider benefits for the Argentine economy but merely acted as funnels to drain wealth to the ports and out of the country. The fact that the rail lines tended to radiate out from the city of Buenos Aires has led Corradi [1974] to argue that this development served to reinforce the economic domination of the littoral. Lewis [1977] attacks these interpretations, claiming that the particular pattern of expansion was the result of nothing more than topographical factors and that the railways served to enhance, but did not initiate, the country's export orientation. He further denies that the British companies conspired to ensure Argentine export dominance but concedes that 'because of their linkages with the export sector, the railways permitted the rapid growth and easy operation of an "open" economic system that inhibited a more balanced pattern of economic development' [*426*]. Except for the idea of planned coercion, which figures only in the writings of the cruder *dependentistas*, views on the effects of railway development seem remarkably similar.

IMMIGRATION

Of all the Latin American countries, Argentina not only attracted the largest absolute number of immigrants (Table XV) in the period under review, but her population also had a greater proportion of foreigners. In 1914, about 30 per cent of the population was foreign-born (coming mainly from Italy and Spain), and among adults in Buenos Aires the figure was 75 per cent. Although organised recruitment was undertaken by the state, direct subsidies

Table xiv
Argentine Railways (km) and Control 1884–1929

	km	British companies (km and % controlled)
1884	3000	–
1894	12,704	–
1900	16,450	14,093 (85.7%)
1909	23,854	18,107 (75.9%)
1915	33,494	24,051 (71.8%)
1929	36,440	25,064 (68.8%)

Sources: Ford, 1975, p. 17; Lewis, 1977, p. 415.

Table xv
Net Immigration into Argentina 1857–1930

1857–60	11,000	1891–1900	320,000
1861–70	77,000	1901–10	1,120,000
1871–80	85,000	1911–20	269,000
1881–90	638,000	1921–30	856,000

Source: Diaz-Alejandro, 1970, p. 421.

were never very important, for cheap fares and propaganda offering the prospect of a better life were sufficient attraction. Of the country's need for immigrants, Solberg writes, 'Perhaps the most common theme of the pro-immigration ideology was that rapid economic development required vast numbers of foreign laborers' [Solberg, 1970, 25]. He also observes that many of the Argentine elite believed, and found justification in contemporary European theories of biological determinism, that the native *mestizo* was racially inferior. 'White' immigration was therefore needed, so it was claimed, if the nation was to progress and become truly civilised.

Turning finally to the question of the overall consequences of export-led growth for Argentina it is not surprising that the division of opinion is similar to that on Brazil, although those exposing an 'optimistic' analysis are on far stronger ground with respect to Argentina. One of the most detailed, cogent arguments for the essentially beneficial nature of export-oriented development is made by Diaz-Alejandro. He points out that by 1929 Argentina was the world's eleventh most important trading nation, real Gross Domestic Product had grown by the substantial annual rate of 4.8 per cent between 1900 and 1929, and the foundations had been laid for the development of manufacturing industry. Furthermore, over these years there was a substantial improvement in living standards; real wages rose, death and infant mortality rates declined, and illiteracy had been reduced from 77 per cent in 1869 (14 years old and upwards) to only 25 per cent in 1929. He writes, 'On the whole the great expansion of 1860–1930 benefited to a smaller or larger extent all major groups connected with the Argentine economy – native and immigrant workers, urban capitalists, foreign investors and even . . . the British working class' [Diaz-Alejandro, 1970, 50].

Diaz-Alejandro maintains that in broad terms pre-1930 Argentina fits into the pattern of development suggested by the staple theory of growth, in other words that the progressive transformation of an economy can be achieved, under certain conditions, through the expansion of primary product exports. This thesis is advanced strongly by Gallo [1971] with respect to industrialisation, which as suggested above is often taken as a sign of meaningful development. He begins by questioning the key assumption that a basic conflict existed between large landowners and industrialists and that the economic and political dominance of the former forestalled industrialisation. He claims there was no such conflict, that industry benefited from protective tariffs from 1876, and that in fact by 1920 industry had achieved a significant level of development. Furthermore, this development relied greatly on the continued successful expansion of the export sector both for generating income and therefore demand and for maintaining the capacity to import capital goods and raw materials. He observes, for example, that during the first world war when the external sector was disrupted the industrial growth rate declined. Geller[9] and Gravil [1977] present similar

67

assessments of Argentine development during this period, and these closely parallel the arguments of Dean and others on the Brazilian experience.

A very different view is taken by Ferrer, Scobie and Di Tella and Zymelman, who maintain, albeit from distinct analytical perspectives, that the continued domination of the agricultural interests stood as a major obstacle to more dynamic industrial development. Di Tella and Zymelman see this as a problem only from about 1914, for they argue that until then agrarian expansion had played a positive role in laying down the 'preconditions' for the country's economic development. By the first world war manufacturing industry accounted for between 11.5 and 15.6 per cent of GDP [Diaz-Alejandro, 1970, *10*], but many of the modern, large-scale factories, such as meat-packing plants and tanneries, were adjuncts of the export sector and entirely dependent upon it. Firms supplying goods for the domestic market remained generally small and inefficient. As a rough indication of the weakness of this sector, in the period 1925–9 37 per cent of imports were consumer goods [Diaz-Alejandro, 1970, *15*] compared with only 21 per cent in Brazil (1920–9) [Villela and Suzigan, 1977, *128*]. Commenting on the nature of Argentine industrial development by the first world war Scobie writes [1964, *Argentina, 177*], 'this was not industrialisation that necessarily promised balanced growth or economic independence. Initially, industrial expansion acquired neither the volume nor the direction commensurate with the impetus of the agricultural revolution.' Although generally there seems to have been a positive correlation between export expansion and industrial growth, as in the case of Brazil, the character and strength of the industrial sector remains in doubt. Did it provide the basis for sustained development and wider social transformation, or was the industry which emerged simply another facet of the country's dependent economic structure?

Laclau [1969] sums up the overall problem rather well when he writes, 'If the index of underdevelopment is measured by the low level of per capita income, Argentina cannot be so classified. If on the other hand, we analyse the nature of her insertion in the world market, we cannot but observe the vulnerable and dependent character of her entire economic structure.'

5 Peru

INDEPENDENCE

WHILE the rest of the Spanish empire was being convulsed by internal struggles for independence, Peru, where royalist sentiment was overwhelmingly dominant, became a base for launching counter-revolutionary incursions into neighbouring countries. This was because Peru was the principal seat of Spanish authority in South America, and, despite the adverse effects of the Bourbon Reforms (for example, the ending of Lima's trade monopoly and the loss of the mines of Upper Peru), the creole elite's prosperity had been built on their relatively privileged position. They did not want to put this position at risk, and at the same time they feared social unrest. Their alarm was fully justified, for the predominantly Indian and *mestizo* population over whom this small white elite ruled had on numerous occasions shown itself prepared to seek redress for its grievances in bloody uprisings. The most famous of these was the Tupac Amaru Rebellion of the 1780s. It was only after the landing in 1820 of a 'liberation army' from Chile led by San Martin that a locally based independence movement began to take shape. Even then its progress was slow and unsure, requiring in 1823 yet further outside intervention, this time from the north under the leadership of Simon Bolivar. Although Peruvian independence was formally declared in 1821, it was not until 1824 at the Battle of Ayacucho that the main body of royalist forces was defeated. The last Spanish troops on the continent finally surrendered in January 1826 at Callao.

THE ERA OF GUANO

Hunt [1973] offers a useful periodisation of Peru's economic performance in the century following independence: 1) Post-Independence Recovery (1826–40), 2) Early Guano Age (1841–9), 3) Mature Guano Age (1850–78), 4) Invasion and Collapse (1879–81), 5) Slow Recovery (1881–95) and 6) New Export Economy (1895–1930). Of all these periods, none has interested historians as much as the Guano Age, because the promise of economic development held out by the dramatic expansion of exports was so great and the final results so disappointing. For this reason, and because guano provides a particularly interesting example of export growth, most of this abbreviated case study is given over to the much debated question of guano and economic growth in Peru.

As in most other regions, independence did not bring fundamental changes to Peru's social and economic structures. The principal legacies of the war years were political chaos, physical destruction and economic dislocation. The mines, the mainstay of the colonial export economy, were in ruins, as was the fairly extensive slave-based agricultural sector which had developed in the fertile river valleys of Peru's otherwise arid coastal strip. Moreover, capital flowed out of the country and foreign merchants rushed in, soon to dominate what was left of Peru's foreign trade. Because of these factors, the country's small, impoverished domestic market and the long history of export dependence, it is hardly surprising that in the post-independence period the export sector should once again assume a dominant role.

Commenting on a major feature of the change from colony to republic, José Carlos Mariátegui [1971, 10] wrote, 'It is interesting that in the story of the republic such coarse and humble substances as guano and nitrates should have taken over the role that had been reserved to gold and silver in a more romantic and less positivist era.' Guano was indeed 'coarse and humble', being excreted by millions of sea birds on Peru's small offshore islands. Because it virtually never rains on the coast, the nitrogen, for which guano was especially prized as a fertilizer, was not leached away, and until the 1870s when other sources of supply, including Peruvian nitrates, began to appear on the market, Peru had a virtual monopoly of the world's supply of nitrogenous fertilizer.

Peruvian guano differed in almost all important respects from the general run of nineteenth-century primary exports. First, it did not have to be produced or processed, but was simply dug out and loaded into waiting ships. This required little more than picks, shovels and wheelbarrows. No railways, ports, or storage facilities were needed. Furthermore, very little labour was required, on average from 600 to 800 workmen, mainly badly paid indentured Chinese [Mathew, 1977]. Secondly, guano was wholly owned by the state, which contracted for its loading and export and which derived by far the largest proportion of the receipts from its sale. Over the almost four decades from 1840, about 12 million tons were exported, realising over 750 million pesos [Hunt, 1973]. On the strength of these earnings Peru had become by 1875 the single largest Latin American government borrower on the London market (£33,535,000 or 26 per cent of the total loaned to governments). None the less, when the guano boom finally collapsed in the 1870s it seemed that Peru had little to show in terms of economic development for forty years of export growth. Why was this so?

Of all the modern accounts of Peru's guano episode, possibly the most influential has been that of Levin [1960]. He deals with a wide range of issues, but three of his arguments are of particular interest. Firstly, he maintains that the contractors who sold the guano on consignment for the government engaged in various dubious and dishonest practices which reduced government receipts. Besides outright fraud, the contractors inflated loading and sales costs, on which they earned a percentage, and they also tended to sell guano at low prices, against the long-term interests of Peru, because they earned a commission on gross sales. These accusations have fostered the widely accepted view that during these years foreign consignees systematically robbed Peru of its export wealth. Secondly, Levin argues that in 1849 under strong pressure from the British government Peru was forced to consolidate and renew payment on loans which had been in default since the mid-1820s. In this way, 'the London bondholders (thus) became major partners in the Peruvian guano business' [63]. Finally, Levin contends that the wider impact of guano on the economy was limited because all the factors needed for production – capital, labour and entrepreneurship – were imported. Furthermore, there was a substantial drain of income to foreign bondholders, and those Peruvians who profited from the trade were a small group of Lima capitalists which 'very early acquired expensive tastes and directed the greatest part of its income – and of Peru's guano-trade proceeds – to the consumption of luxuries' [117]. Levin puts forward the Peruvian experience as a classic example of enclave development, in which the export sector has few links with the domestic economy. Broad-based economic change accordingly was not set in motion.

Both of Levin's arguments have come under attack. Mathew [1981], basing his work on the papers of Antony Gibbs & Sons, Peru's principal guano consignees from 1842 to 1861, shows conclusively that although certain of Gibbs's activities can be criticised, fraudulent practices were not particularly significant and that on the whole there was no conflict of interests between Gibbs and the government over costs and prices. He also questions Levin's notion that foreigners dominated the trade because of their superior commercial acumen or because their capital was needed to establish the infrastructure for guano production. Rather, it was the government's incessant need to borrow money in advance of sales which made the financially well-connected foreign merchant houses so attractive. Moreover, for Mathew the 1849 debt settlement was prompted by Peru's desire to have access to the London capital market rather than by British government pressure. He judges the latter to have been relatively unimportant [Mathew, 1970]. He goes on to challenge the assumption that Gibbs encouraged borrowing so as to increase its hold over the government. The demand for advances came from various administrations anxious to increase their immediate spending power. Because the economic and political structure of the country was not sufficiently stable or sophisticated the loans which guano revenue underwrote were on the whole used unproductively. Mathew concludes,

> Guano exporting was, in the last resort, in the hands of insecure and inadequately-financed governments, operating within a shaky immature body politic. Such governments manifested, over guano, a paradoxical combination of power and penury. The penury dictated the way in which the power was used; and the power being badly used, served in the end to aggravate the penury. [Mathew, 1981, *246*]

Hunt directs his criticisms at Levin's use of the guano trade as an example of enclave development. In the first place over 60 per cent of the income (a figure which Mathew considers too low) went directly to the government. He estimates that in four decades the overall value retained by the economy was between 65 and 71 per cent of final sales. Furthermore, he claims that only 8 per cent and $11\frac{1}{2}$ per cent of the government's guano earnings went to pay off respectively foreign and local creditors, and because benefits from the trade were more widely distributed than is generally believed, demand was created for domestically produced goods and services. All this makes guano for Hunt the very opposite of an enclave. Nonetheless, there was scant progressive change within Peru, and Hunt ascribes this to the fact that little productive effort was needed to make money from guano. As a consequence Peru became a 'rentier economy, exporting guano and importing virtually all manufactured goods' [Hunt, 1973, *105*]. The point about imports is questioned by Mathew [1981], and it does seem to contradict Hunt's own claim that guano earnings stimulated demand for domestic production. Also, while the income retained in Peru seems to have been substantial, the extremely primitive nature of guano extraction [Mathew, 1977] meant there were almost no productive or demand linkages established with the rest of the economy. In this sense the guano trade was an exemplary case of enclave development.

Although assessments differ considerably, the general consensus seems to be that the guano age was a time of failure and missed opportunity. There were, however, some 'positive' features of the period which should at least be mentioned. Guano income flowed directly and indirectly (through the various banks set up from the 1860s) into the improvement of coastal agriculture, including the building of short rail lines and ports. Cotton exports rose from about 300 metric tons (mt) in 1855 to a peak of 5640 mt in 1872, while sugar showed a more dramatic expansion, increasing from 1150 mt in 1855 to 83,500 mt in 1879. Further, by the 1860s nitrate exports from the far south of the country began to expand vigorously, promising to replace the guano trade which began to fade from 1870. Finally, there were government efforts to use guano revenue to finance an ambitious, but on the whole ill-conceived, programme of railway-construction across the Andes. The various projects, plagued by financial and engineering difficulties, were finally overtaken by events. In 1875 there was a major financial crisis, due in no small measure to the massive debts contracted to support rail-building. Construction was brought to a halt, and a year later the government was forced to suspend payment on its considerable foreign debts. The era was brought to a definitive end by the outbreak of the War of the Pacific in 1879, fought over the rich nitrate fields in the Atacama Desert, and in which Bolivia and Peru were decisively defeated by Chile.

1883–1930

In 1878 nitrate and guano accounted for 65 per cent of Peru's exports, the richest guano deposits were already exhausted, and when the occupying Chilean forces withdrew in 1883, the nitrate fields were under their control. It took some time for other export sectors to recover. From 1895, however, their rate of growth was spectacular, averaging almost 20 per cent a year to 1900. With significant fluctuations, the indices of both the quantum and value of exports grew at about 7 per cent per annum, between 1890 and 1920. An important aspect of this apparently vigorous development was that, unlike the pre-war years, there was now a wide range of export commodities (Table xvi), making the economy less vulnerable to specific adverse market changes. A less auspicious new departure was the substantial increase in direct foreign control. This took a number of forms. In order to settle her large outstanding foreign debt Peru was obliged in 1890 to sign the Grace Contract. This established the British-run Peruvian Corporation to which the government turned over almost all the country's railways, granting in addition a yearly lump-sum payment and the right to exploit the remaining guano deposits [Miller, 1976]. Besides the domination by foreign merchants of the import–export trade, by the first world war both mining and petroleum were in the hands of large foreign corporations.

Klarén [1977, *229*] expresses a widely accepted view when he writes that from 1890, 'Anglo-American investment capital (combined direct investment grew from \$17 million in 1880 to \$209 million by 1929) gradually carved out the export enclaves in sugar, cotton, copper, oil, and other raw materials which today are familiar features of the Peruvian economic landscape.' This is not, however, entirely accurate, for agricultural exports remained predominantly in local hands, with only a few large sugar estates being foreign owned [Albert, 1976; Thorp and Bertram, 1978]. The problem was that cotton and sugar went into decline in the late 1920s leaving foreigners in control of the most dynamic export sectors. Because of this Thorp and Bertram conclude that,

the net impact of foreign capital on Peruvian growth up to 1930 was negative – on balance, it is in our judgement probable that the economy would have reached a higher level of GNP by 1930 without foreign capital than with it.

[Thorp and Bertram, 1978, *143*]

Table XVI

Composition of Peruvian Exports by Value (percentage, share) 1895–1930

	Sugar	Cotton	Wool	Silver	Copper	Rubber	Petroleum
1895	35	7	15	26	1	14	–
1910	20	14	7	10	18	18	2
1920	42	30	2	5	7	1	5
1925	11	32	4	10	8	1	24
1930	11	18	3	4	10	–	30

Source: Thorp and Bertram, 1978, p. 40.

In comparison with Brazil or Argentina, Peru did rather badly out of her external links (see Table V). There were changes, but substantial progressive development – including the growth of industry – was not in evidence by 1930. This had much to do with internal social and political conditions, but was exacerbated by the increasing degree of direct control exercised by foreigners over the Peruvian economy in the 1920s, which meant that a large proportion of the export earnings was drawn out of the country and domestic capital accumulation thereby made more difficult.

INDEPENDENCE

IT was not until 1789 that the separate Captaincy-General of Chile was created, the country having been throughout the preceding years a dominated outpost of the Viceroyalty of Peru. This subservient position engendered resentment towards her northern rulers, fostered a distinctive sense of regional identity, and helps explain the relative weakness of royalist support here as compared with Peru during the struggle for independence. From 1818 Spanish power was effectively broken, and until 1823 the country was under the firm hand of the hero of the liberation, Bernardo O'Higgins. After his overthrow there ensued a period of bitter conflict between liberal and conservative forces which ended in the latter's victory and the establishment of an authoritarian regime masterminded by Diego Portales. This was both reactionary and repressive, but the republic set up under the 1833 Constitution was also extremely durable and lasted, with the interruption of only two short-lived rebellions in 1851 and 1859, until 1891. Through both its 'autocratic' (1833–61) and 'liberal' (1861–91) phases there was an ordered, peaceful, presidential succession. Political stability of this sort was remarkable in nineteenth-century Latin America and for that matter anywhere else in the world.

Most economic historians divide the years 1830–1930 into two main sub-periods, corresponding roughly to two major export cycles. The first to the 1870s was characterised by the growth of mining and wheat exports, while the second from the War of the Pacific was dominated by the nitrate trade.

1830–79

The political stability imposed from the 1830s underlay, and was in its turn strengthened by, a dramatic increase in exports (Table xvii), most significantly from the mines of the *norte chico* region (see map). New silver workings were found and opened up from the early decades of the century, but a major strike at Chañarcillo in 1832 was the key to a very rapid expansion in output. The growth in copper mining was even more impressive, and by the 1860s Chile accounted for about 40 per cent of world production. Although there was substantial British investment in copper, by and large

Table XVII
Chilean Exports 1844–77

| | Average value of total exports (£000) | Percentage share | | | |
		Copper	Silver	Wheat & Barley	Flour
1844–7	1398	37	28	5	6
1854–7	4499	36	21	7	10
1864–7	5275	37	14	19	–
1874–7	6278	50	12	16	–

Sources: *Estadística Comercial de la República de Chile 1844–1847, Anuario Estadístico de la República de Chile 1860, Sinopsis Estadística de la República de Chile 1924.* For the first two periods total exports includes re-exports, although the percentages have been calculated on 'national' exports.

both types of mining ventures were locally owned. Among other things, the growth of mining encouraged migration into the region, stimulated agricultural production, and led to the construction of Chile's first railways.

The other main exports in this period were wheat and flour. These came in the first instance from the central valleys and subsequently also from the southern frontier region, where to facilitate agrarian expansion the Araucanian Indians were forcibly expelled. The gold rushes in California and Australia are often cited as having provided the impetus for the growth of grain exports, but although prices were driven up to extremely high levels, demand from these areas was relatively short-lived. Of more enduring importance was the traditional Peruvian market and the opening of European markets, particularly that of Britain from the mid-1860s. Bauer [1975] observes that a combination of high prices, falling freight costs, and the fact that at this time Chile was the only large-scale exporter of wheat from the southern hemisphere, underpinned the country's export success between 1866 and 1880.

Although mining and agriculture greatly expanded their output and enjoyed export success in these years, in both cases it was done without forcing any major changes in productive techniques or organisation. Mining was so prosperous primarily because new, rich deposits were exploited, and in agriculture greater output was achieved by the relatively simple expedient of expanding acreage. Therefore when world prices of the three major exports began to fall in the early 1870s producers found it difficult to reduce costs quickly enough. The result was severe economic crisis throughout the economy.

There seems to be broad agreement that the expansion of exports led to considerable economic advance in these years. An important debate has, however, developed over the question of export earnings and attempts at state-directed economic development. It is argued that during the administrations of presidents Prieto, Bulnes and Montt (1830–61) there were concerted efforts to harness the country's export wealth, and with this to control, or at the very least to influence, the course of economic change. Among other measures, this involved protective tariffs for industry, policies designed to enlarge Chile's merchant fleet, and state-sponsored improvements of ports, roads, education and the construction of railways and telegraph lines. According to historians like Jobet, Ramirez, Encina and Pinto, by the 1860s the leaders of this more nationalist programme were pushed from power by an emergent bourgeoisie embued with a doctrinaire liberal ideology.[10] The latter group sought to limit the role of the state and at the same time began to dismantle the system of protective tariffs and regulations.' Frank [1969], drawing on the work of these writers, claims that in this way Chile was drawn more firmly into the international capitalist system as an economic satellite of Britain, resulting in the deepening and reinforcing of the country's structural underdevelopment.

This interpretation has been seriously questioned in recent years. For example, in his study of Chile's merchant marine, Véliz[11] argues that the Ordinance of 1864, which is generally blamed for causing the destruction of the Chilean fleet by allowing foreign ships into the coastal trade, was in fact not all that important. He shows that foreign shipping had been able to evade Chilean restrictions from 1849, and that furthermore after the war with Spain (1865–6) the country's merchant tonnage increased. Sater [1976] maintains that the more liberal trade policies introduced in 1864 were being reversed by 1869, and that protection was stepped up thereafter. Ortega [forthcoming] takes this argument somewhat further and points out that over the entire period tariffs were primarily fiscal weapons, industrial protection always being a secondary consideration. Finally, Sunkel and Cariola [1978] show that government projects, such as railway-building, port-improvement, begun under the pre-1860 administrations were continued in the following period. The available evidence suggests that these analyses are in general the more tenable in this particular debate. Nevertheless, it is clear as Frank and others insist that the fortunes of the Chilean economy were tied firmly to the vagaries of the world market, creating problems of stability. Further, while locals controlled the majority of export production, as elsewhere, commerce relied almost entirely on foreign merchants and from 1865 foreign capital also became more important (see Table 1). These twin problems of external vulnerability and economic domination were to persist.

1880–1930

At the same time as Chile's main export sectors went into decline, new mineral wealth was being developed to the north in the Chilean, Peruvian and Bolivian provinces of the Atacama Desert. Nitrate, used in industry and in agriculture as a fertilizer, had been exploited from the 1830s, but it was not until the 1860s that its export began to assume major importance. There were continued conflicts between the three countries, particularly as borders in certain areas were disputed. Also foreign capitalists were prominent in the region, and in the Bolivian province of Antofagasta economic life was dominated by Chilean entrepreneurs and workers. To complicate matters further, from 1875 Peru had been in the process of nationalising the nitrate fields and *oficinas* (plants for processing nitrate) in its province of Tarapaca, the major producing area. The causes of the war which eventualy broke out in 1879 are still disputed. For many years it had been assumed that it had been fermented by foreign powers anxious to overturn Peruvian nationalisation, but Kiernan [1955] found no evidence to support this charge. In a more recent work, O'Brien [1980] argues that 'The three nations were long and bitter rivals and a serious economic decline in Chile since the mid-1870s had conditioned the nation's elite to accept warfare as a possible escape from crisis'. Whatever the underlying causes, the spark which ignited the conflict was a

Table XVIII
Chilean Exports 1884–1929

	Average value of total exports (£000)	Percentage share			
		Nitrate & Iodine	Copper	Silver	Wheat & Barley
1884–93	9966	49	20	11	4
1894–1903	12,393	64	12	–	4
1904–13	23,347	75	8	–	3
1914–23	37,497	66	16	–	–
1924–29	46,981	56	28	–	–

Sources: *Sinopsis Estadística de la República de Chile 1924; Statesmen's Yearbook 1927 and 1930.*

dispute between Bolivia and Chile over taxation. Once hostilities had started Peru joined Bolivia, honouring a secret mutual defence treaty. The war resulted in a Chilean victory and a takeover of the entire region just at the time when it was reaching a high point in its export development.

The following years were dominated by the question of nitrate. The figures in Table XVIII show why this was the case. Two issues will be considered here: the causes and significance of the civil war or counter-revolution of 1891, widely thought to have been a battle over the foreign control of the nitrate fields, and secondly, the broader problem of the effect of nitrate exports on the country's economic development.

Although Chile may have fought to capture the nitrate fields, in the years after the War of the Pacific Chilean capital was left with a much reduced share of the productive basis. For example, British ownership of *oficinas* rose from 13 per cent in 1878 to 70 per cent by 1890, and four years later 92 per cent of the industry's output came from foreign-owned companies [Greenhill, 1977]. Foreign takeovers were on the increase before the war, but the sudden rise after 1883 came because Chile gave in to pressure and honoured the bonds given to the nitrate producers by Peru during the pre-war nation-alisation drive. As most of these securities had been bought up at extremely low prices by a British consortium headed by John T. North, the so-called 'Nitrate King', many of the most productive nitrate fields in Tarapaca were soon in his hands. North and his associates also owned, among other ventures, the Bank of London and Tarapaca, the Tarapaca Waterworks Co. (a key concession in the desert), and the Nitrate Railways Co., which had an absolute monopoly of transport in the Tarapaca nitrate field.

Many historians have maintained that it is against this background of overwhelming foreign domination of the country's major export that the policies and eventual overthrow of President José Manuel Balmaceda (1886–91) must be understood. Ramirez[12] has argued that Balmaceda wanted to use the nitrate revenues (exports were heavily taxed) in a broad programme of national development, and foreign control represented an obstacle to the success of his plans. This led him into conflict with the nitrate producers, most specifically North and his Nitrate Railway Co., and then with the Congress over a constitutional issue relating to the railway's monopoly privileges. This complex situation resulted in a bitter civil war, Balmaceda's defeat and his subsequent suicide. He is seen as a man who tried to alter the course of Chile's development by freeing it from the domination of foreign capital. His defeat was a victory for the forces of imperialism and its Chilean collaborators.

A number of scholars have questioned this view. Loveman [1979] for example, comments that although Balmaceda's plans were ambitious, he was not all that radical and did not seek to take over or even discourage foreign capital. Blakemore [1974] claims that the civil war was not fought over economic issues, but was essentially a constitutional conflict between the President and Congress. While he makes many extremely telling points Blakemore's interpretation is limited by a narrowness of conception which could be said to characterise the entire controversy. As Monteon [1975] has argued, whoever won the civil war, Britain's economic domination – through shipping, commerce, finance and its control of the most productive nitrate fields – would have continued, and in terms of Chile's economic prospects this was the major consideration.

Opinion varies considerably on the question of the overall impact of nitrate and foreign intervention on Chile's development. Few writers take as rosy a view as Mamalakis [1976], who sees the nitrate era as one of rapid and substantial progress. Sunkel and Cariola [1978], while recognising the deficiencies of Chilean capitalism, write, 'the expansion of the nitrate export activity, even though controlled to a great extent by foreign capital, far from being an isolated enclave which inhibited capitalist development in Chile, was on the contrary a fundamental factor in its expansion' [vi]. This offers a direct challenge to Frank's belief [1969] that nitrates served to enrich the metropolis and underdevelop Chile. Not only is this latter interpretation rather crude, but more importantly it does not seem to reflect what actually took place in Chile. Far more considered and valuable analyses are provided in the works of Bauer [1975], Kirsch [1977] and O'Brien [1980]. Although both their approaches and findings differ, they all agree that the main drawback of dependence on nitrate revenue was that because it was tapped and distributed by the state it did not produce a class able to transform the country's traditional social and economic order. As Bauer writes, 'The nitrate fields produced a torrent of wealth but paradoxically this went to fortify an elite whose principal value was still landownership' [229].

A final word has to be said about the growth of US interest in Chile, an interest which became pronounced from the turn of the century. US investment increased from $15 million in 1913 to almost $620 million in 1928 (see Table iv). The most significant feature of this was the takeover of Chile's major copper mines, revived by a new technical process introduced from 1900 which allowed the economic recovery of low-grade ores. By 1920 80 per cent of the country's copper output was being produced by two large US firms, and by 1928 copper was responsible for 32 per cent of the country's export earnings [Reynolds, 1965]. This percentage was to increase in the years that followed as the production of synthetics destroyed the market for nitrates. Just at a time when the Chilean participation in nitrate production was increasing, the country's leading export sector fell once again to foreign capital, and the economic and political problems this was to help create were to have tragic consequences.

7 Conclusion

THE diversity of experience of four countries which were subjected to many of the same outside influences underlines the analytical limitations of studies such as this which concentrate so heavily on external factors. Of course, trade, foreign investment and immigration need to be investigated, but more attention must be given to how they affected and were affected by the course of political and social change within each country. The case studies also suggest that the *dependentista* challenge to the liberal diffusionist view of economic and social change has not been adequately supported by substantive historical research. For example, there is little evidence that in post-independence Latin America there were genuine opportunities for relatively autonomous, self-generating economic development. Furthermore, a study of the first world war period indicates that at least for Brazil and Argentina export growth and links with the international economy encouraged rather than hindered industrial development. It also appears that contrary to Frank's theses of stagnation and the 'creation of underdevelopment' there was a very substantial degree of materially progressive change in many parts of Latin America in the century before 1930. Finally, although more research is called for, it seems doubtful whether there was a drain of wealth from the area because of long-term deterioration in the terms of trade.

This apparent rout of the dependency argument has occurred because those who have advocated it, mainly sociologists and political scientists, have been principally concerned with elaborating and refining their theories, not with testing and amending their historical hypotheses.[13] This has made it relatively easy for traditional historians, who somewhat smugly pride themselves on their empirical hardheadedness, to dismiss these hypotheses as little more than fanciful speculations. However, it would be wrong to reject the entire dependency approach on these grounds, for most of the specific criticisms levelled against it by historians are directed at Frank's early writings and these have also come under sustained and comprehensive attack from other *dependentistas* [O'Brien, 1975]. Nonetheless, the value of dependency as a broad framework within which to understand historical change has yet to be convincingly demonstrated in practice. So far both its proponents and its detractors have treated it mainly as a set of fixed concepts to be proved or disproved, attacked or defended. This polemical exercise has generated a lot of heat but much less light.

While historians will continue to argue about their character and significance it is abundantly clear that far-reaching economic, social and political changes took place throughout most of Latin America in the century following independence. Many of the most significant of these changes were the result of links forged with the expanding world capitalist system, links which simultaneously advanced and ensnared, to varying degrees, the economies of the new nations. The difficulties imposed by external vulnerability and foreign economic domination in the years to 1930 might seem to be relatively insignificant when compared to the levels of material progress achieved in some countries. Or they may seem as merely the type of short- and medium-term problems invariably associated with fundamental socio-economic transformation. However, not only is the character and extent of this transformation in doubt, but it is also clear that the difficulties experienced, far from being transitory phenomena, were symptomatic of more deep-seated weaknesses in the economic, social and political structures upon which export-led growth and 'progress' had been built. This was to become increasingly apparent in the decades that followed.

Despite the substantial industrial development eventually achieved in some countries, notably Mexico, Brazil and Argentina, extreme susceptibility to external disequilibrium and foreign economic control are abiding problems throughout most of Latin America because of massive foreign debts, continued reliance on primary exports and the pervasive and generally perverse influence of multinational firms. Moreover, the essential weakness of capitalism here has made it increasingly difficult, especially in the economically more advanced countries, for the state to contain class conflict without resorting to the type of unconscionably brutal, systematic repression characteristic of the regimes which now rule in Argentina, Brazil, Chile and Uruguay. The reasons for the rise of this new form of authoritarianism have still to be clearly delineated.[14] However, a key part of the explanation is to be found in an analysis of the socio-economic structures formed in the process of Latin America's incorporation into the modern world capitalist system and in an understanding of how, through a combination of external pressure and domestic class struggle, these structures were transformed over time [Cardoso and Faletto, 1979]. An appreciation of these questions is essential to any critical assessment of the nature and diversity of socio-economic change in Latin America up to and after 1930.

Notes

1 F. H. Cardoso, 'The Consumption of Dependency Theory in the United States', *Latin American Research Review*, XII, 3 (1977) 15.

2. D. C. M. Platt, 'The Imperialism of Free Trade: Some Reservations', *Economic History Review*, 2nd series, XXI, 2 (1968) 297.

3 R. A. White, 'The Denied Revolution: Paraguay's Economics of Independence', *Latin American Perspectives*, VI, 2 (1979) 21.

4 Raul Prebisch, *The Economic Development of Latin America and its Principal Problems* (New York, 1950).

5 S. B. Saul, *Studies in British Overseas Trade 1870–1914* (Liverpool, 1960) pp. 14–15, 221–2.

6 G. L. Beckford, *Persistent Poverty: Underdevelopment in Plantation Economies of the Third World* (London, 1972).

7 R. Hilton (ed.), *The Transition from Feudalism to Capitalism* (London, 1976).

8 J. P. Calogeras, *A History of Brazil* (trans., Chapel Hill, 1939) 191.

9 L. Geller, 'El crecimiento industrial argentino hasta 1914 y la teoria del bien primario exportable', *El Trimestre Economico*, XXXVII, 148 (1970).

10 S. Collier, 'The Historiography of the Portalian Period 1830–1891 in Chile', *Hispanic American Historical Review*, LVI (1977).

11 C. Véliz, *Historía de la Marina Mercente de Chile* (Santiago, 1961).

12 H. Ramirez Necochea, *Balmaceda y la Contrarevolucion de 1891* (2nd edn, Santiago, 1969).

13 See for example 'Dependency and Marxism', a special issue of *Latin American Perspectives*, VIII, 3 and 4 (1981).

14 David Collier (ed.), *The New Authoritarianism in Latin America* (Princeton, 1979).

Select Bibliography

REFERENCE AND JOURNALS

The Handbook of Latin American Studies, yearly from 1936. Invaluable, giving brief notes on most recent publications.

Cortés Conde, R. and Stein, S. J., *Latin America: A Guide to Economic History* (Berkeley, 1977). Annotated bibliographies and historiographical essays on Argentina, Brazil, Chile, Peru, Mexico and Colombia.

The principal journals in English are:

Bulletin of Latin American Research [BLAR] 1981–
Hispanic American Historical Review [HAHR] 1918–
Inter-American Economic Affairs [IAEA] 1947–
Journal of Latin American Studies [JLAS] 1969–
Latin American Perspectives [LAP] 1974–
Latin American Research Review [LARR] 1966–

GENERAL STUDIES

Albert, B. and Henderson, P., 'Latin America and the Great War: A Preliminary Survey of Developments in Chile, Peru, Argentina, and Brazil' *World Development* IX, 8 (Aug. 1981).

Cardoso, F. H. and Faletto, E., *Dependency and Development in Latin America* (Berkeley, 1979).

Chilcote, R. H. and Edelstein, J. C., *Latin America: the Struggle with Dependency and Beyond* (Cambridge, Mass., 1974).

Cortés Conde, R., *The First Stages of Modernization in Spanish America* (New York, 1974).

Duncan, K. and Rutledge, I. (eds), *Land and Labour in Latin America* (Cambridge, 1977).

Frank, A. G., *Capitalism and Underdevelopment in Latin America: Historical Studies of Chile and Brazil* (New York, 1969).

——————, *Lumpen-Bourgeoisie: Lumpendevelopment* (New York, 1972).

Furtado, C., *Economic Development in Latin America* (Cambridge, 1970).

Greenhill, R., 'Merchants and the Latin American Trades: an Introduction', in D. C. M. Platt (ed.), *Business Imperialism* (Oxford, 1977).

Halperín-Donghi, T., *The Aftermath of Revolution in Latin America* (New York, 1973).

Joslin, D., *A Century of Banking in Latin America* (London, 1963).

Laclau (h.), E., 'Feudalism and Capitalism in Latin America', *New Left Review*, LXVII (1971).

Lewis, C. and Abel, C. (eds), *The Latin American Experience of Economic Imperialism* (London, forthcoming).

Lynch, J., *The Spanish American Revolutions, 1808–1826* (New York, 1973).

Miller, R., 'Latin American Manufacturing and the First World War: an Exploratory Essay', *World Development* IX, 8 (Aug. 1981).

O'Brien, P. J., 'A Critique of Latin American Theories of Dependency', in I. Oxaal, T. Barnett and D. Booth (eds), *Beyond the Sociology of Development* (London, 1975).

Platt, D. C. M., *Finance, Trade and Politics in British Foreign Policy 1815–1914* (Oxford, 1968).

—————, *Latin America and British Trade 1806–1914* (London, 1972).

—————(ed.), *Business Imperialism 1840–1930: An Inquiry Based on British Experience in Latin America* (Oxford, 1977).

—————, 'Dependency in Nineteenth-Century Latin America: An Historian Objects', *LARR*, xv, 1 (1980).

Rippy, J. F., *British Investments in Latin America, 1822–1949* (Minneapolis, 1959).

Schneider, J., 'Terms of Trade between France and Latin America, 1826–1856: Causes of Increasing Economic Disparities?' in P. Bairoch and M. Levy-Leboyer (eds), *Disparities in Economic Development Since the Industrial Revolution* (London, 1981).

Stein, B. H. and Stein, S. J., *The Colonial Heritage of Latin America* (New York, 1970).

—————, 'D. C. M. Platt: The Anatomy of Autonomy', *LARR*, xv, 1 (1980).

Stone, I., 'British Long-Term Investment in Latin America, 1865–1913', *Business History Review*, XLII, 3 (1968).

United Nations, *Economic Survey of Latin America 1949* (New York, 1951). Valuable study of developments from the mid-1920s. Annual surveys from 1949 onward.

Winkler, M., *Investments of United States Capital in Latin America* (1928, reissue New York, 1971).

Brazil

Bethell, L., *The Abolition of the Brazilian Slave Trade* (Cambridge, 1970).

Coes, D., 'Brazil', in W. Arthur Lewis (ed.), *Tropical Development 1880–1913: Studies in Economic Progress* (London, 1970).

Conrad, R., *The Destruction of Brazilian Slavery 1850–1888* (Berkeley, 1972).

Dean, W., *The Industrialization of São Paulo, 1880–1945* (Austin, 1969).

——————, *Rio Claro: A Brazilian Plantation System, 1820–1920* (Stanford, 1976).

Fishlow, A., 'Origins and Consequences of Import-substitution in Brazil', in Luis E. di Marco (ed.), *International Economics and Development: Essays in Honor of Raul Prebisch* (New York, 1972).

Furtado, C., *The Economic Growth of Brazil* (London, 1963).

Graham, R., *Britain and the Onset of Modernization in Brazil 1850–1914* (Cambridge, 1968).

Greenhill, R., 'The Brazilian Coffee Trade' in D. C. M. Platt (ed.), *Business Imperialism* (Oxford, 1977).

Holloway, T. H., *The Brazilian Coffee Valorization of 1906: Regional Politics and Economic Dependence* (Madison, Wisc., 1975).

——————, *Immigrants on the Land: Coffee and Society in São Paulo, 1886–1934* (Chapel Hill, 1980).

Leff, N., 'Economic Retardation in Nineteenth-Century Brazil', *Economic History Review*, 2nd series, xxv, 4 (1972).

——————, 'Tropical Trade and Development in the Nineteenth Century: The Brazilian Experience', *Journal of Political Economy*, LXXXI (1973).

Manchester, A. K., *British Pre-eminence in Brazil: Its Rise and Decline* (Chapel Hill, 1933).

Mattoon, R. H., Jr., 'Railroads, Coffee and the Growth of Big Business in São Paulo, Brazil', *HAHR*, LVII, 2 (1977).

Normano, J. F., *Brazil: A Study of Economic Types* (Chapel Hill, 1935).

Peláez, C. M., 'The Theory and Reality of Imperialism in the Coffee Economy of Nineteenth-Century Brazil', *Economic History Review*, 2nd series, xxix, 2 (1976).

————, 'World War I and the Economy of Brazil: Some Evidence from Monetary Statistics', *Journal of Interdisciplinary History*, VII, 4 (1977).

Poppino, R. F., *Brazil: The Land and the People* (New York, 1973).

Stein, S. J., *Vassouras: A Brazilian Coffee County, 1850–1900* (Cambridge, Mass., 1957).

————, *The Brazilian Cotton Manufacture: Textile Enterprise in an Underdeveloped Area, 1850–1950* (Cambridge, Mass., 1957).

Versiani, F. R., 'Industrial Investment in an "Export" Economy: The Brazilian Experience before 1914', *Institute of Latin American Studies Working Papers*, no. 2 (London, 1979).

Villela, A. V. and Suzigan, W., *Government Policy and the Economic Growth of Brazil, 1889–1945* (Rio de Janeiro, 1977).

Argentina

Brown, J. C., *A Socioeconomic History of Argentina, 1776–1860* (Cambridge, 1979).

Burgin, M., *Economic Aspects of Argentine Federalism, 1820–1852* (Cambridge, Mass., 1946).

Corradi, J. E., 'Argentina', in R. H. Chilcote and J. C. Edelstein (eds), *Latin America* (1974).

Di Tella, G. and Zymelman, M., *Las etapas del desarrollo economico argentino* (Buenos Aires, 1967).

Diaz-Alejandro, C., *Essays on the Economic History of the Argentine Republic* (New Haven, Conn., 1970).

Ferns, H., *Britain and Argentina in the Nineteenth Century* (Oxford, 1960).

Ferrer, A., *The Argentine Economy* (Berkeley, 1967).

Ford, A. G., *The Gold Standard, 1880–1914: Britain and Argentina* (Oxford, 1962).

————, 'British Investment and Argentine Economic Development 1880–1914' in D. Rock (ed.), *Argentina in the Twentieth Century* (London, 1975).

Gallo, E., 'Agrarian Expansion and Industrial Development in Argentina 1880–1930' in R. Carr (ed.), *Latin American Affairs* (Oxford, 1971).

————, 'The Cereal Boom and Changes in the Social and Political Structure of Santa Fe, Argentina, 1870–95', in K. Duncan and I. Rutledge (eds), *Land and Labour* (1977).

Goodwin, P. B., Jr., 'The Central Argentine Railway and the Economic Development of Argentina, 1854–1881', *HAHR*, LVII, 4 (1977).

Gravil, R., 'The Anglo-Argentine Connection and the War of 1914–1918', *JLAS*, IX, 1 (1977).

Greenhill, R. and Crossley, J. C., 'The River Plate Beef Trade', in D. C. M. Platt (ed.), *Business Imperialism* (Oxford, 1977).

Laclau, E., 'Modos de produción, sistemas económicos y pobleción excedente approximación história a los casos argentino y chileno,' *Revista Latinoamericano de Sociologia*, v, 2 (Santiago, 1969).

Lewis, C., 'British Railway Companies and the Argentine Government', in D. C. M. Platt (ed.), *Business Imperialism* (Oxford, 1977).

——, 'Foreign Investment and the Pattern of Railway Development: the Early Phase of the Railway Age in Brazil and Argentina', in C. Lewis and C. Abel (eds.), *The Latin American Experience* (forthcoming).

Reber, V. B., *British Mercantile Houses in Buenos Aires 1810–1880* (Cambridge, Mass., 1979).

Scobie, J. R., *Argentina: A City and a Nation* (New York, 1964).

——, *Revolution on the Pampas: A Social History of Argentine Wheat, 1860–1910* (Austin, 1964).

Smith, P. H., *Politics and Beef in Argentina: Patterns of Conflict and Change* (New York, 1969).

Solberg, C., *Immigration and Nationalism: Argentina and Chile 1890–1914*, (Austin, 1970).

Vazquez-Presedo, V., *El caso argentino, migración de factores, comercio exterior y desarrollo 1875–1914* (Buenos Aires, 1971).

Peru

Albert, B., *An Essay on the Peruvian Sugar Industry, 1880–1920* (Norwich, 1976).

——, 'External Forces and the Transformation of Peruvian Coastal Agriculture, 1880–1930', in C. Lewis and C. Abel (eds), *The Latin American Experience* (forthcoming).

Bonilla, H., *Guano y Burguesía en el Peru* (Lima, 1974).

Hunt, S. J., 'Growth and Guano in Nineteenth-Century Peru', Discussion Paper no. 31, Woodrow Wilson School Research Program in Economic Development (Princeton, 1973).

Klarén, P., 'The Social and Economic Consequences of Modernization in the Peruvian Sugar Industry, 1870–1930', in K. Duncan and I. Rutledge (eds), *Land and Labour* (Cambridge, 1977).

Levin, J., *The Export Economies: Their Pattern of Development in Historical Perspective* (Cambridge, Mass., 1960).

Mariátegui, J. C., *Seven Interpretative Essays on Peruvian Reality* (Austin, 1971).

Mathew, W. M., 'The First Anglo-Peruvian Debt and its Settlement, 1822–49', *JLAS*, ii, 1 (1970).

————, 'A Primitive Export Sector: Guano Production in Mid-Nineteenth Century Peru', *JLAS*, ix, 1 (1977).

————, *The House of Gibbs and the Peruvian Guano Monopoly* (London, 1981).

Miller, R., 'The Making of the Grace Contract: British Bondholders and the Peruvian Government, 1885–1890', *JLAS*, viii, 1 (1976).

Miller, R. and Greenhill, R., 'The Peruvian Government and the Nitrate Trade, 1873–1879,' *JLAS*, v, 1 (1973).

Stewart, W., *Henry Meiggs: Yankee Pizarro* (Duke, 1946).

————, *Chinese Bondage in Peru: A History of the Chinese Coolie in Peru, 1849–1874* (Duke, 1951).

Thorp, R. and Bertram, G., *Peru 1890–1977: Growth and Policy in an Open Economy* (London, 1978).

Chile

Bauer, A. J., *Chilean Rural Society from the Spanish Conquest to 1930* (Cambridge, 1975).

Blakemore, H., *British Nitrates and Chilean Politics 1886–1896: Balmaceda and North* (London, 1974).

Burr, R. N., *By Reason or Force: Chile and the Balancing of Power in South America, 1830–1905* (Berkeley, 1965).

Greenhill, R., 'The Nitrate and Iodine Trades 1880–1914', in D. C. M. Platt (ed.), *Business Imperialism* (1977).

Kiernan, V. G., 'Foreign Interests in the War of the Pacific', *HAHR*, xxxv (1955).

Kirsch, H. W., *Industrial Development in a Traditional Society: The Conflict of Entrepreneurship and Modernization in Chile* (Gainsville, 1977).

Loveman, B., *Chile: The Legacy of Hispanic Capitalism* (New York, 1979).

Mamalakis, M., *The Growth and Structure of the Chilean Economy: From Independence to Allende* (London, 1976).

Monteon, M., 'The British in the Atacama Desert: The Cultural Bases of Economic Imperialism', *Journal of Economic History*, xxv, 1 (1975).

O'Brien, T., 'The Antofagasta Company: A Case Study of Peripheral Capitalism', *HAHR*, lx, 1 (1980).

Ortega, L., 'Political Economy of Chile in the Half-Century after Independence', in C. Lewis and C. Abel (eds), *The Latin American Experience* (forthcoming).

Reynolds, C., 'Development Problems of an Export Economy: The Case of Chilean Copper', in M. Mamalakis and C. Reynolds, *Essays on the Chilean Economy* (Homewood, Ill., 1965).

Sater, W. F., 'Economic Nationalism and Tax Reform in late Nineteenth-Century Chile', *The Americas*, xxxiii, 2 (1976).

Sunkel, O. and Cariola, C., 'Nitrate Expansion and Socio-Economic Transformation in Chile: 1880–1930', Discussion Paper 129, Institute of Development Studies (Sussex, 1978).

Index

Note: numbers in *Italic* indicate main sections

94